GRENVILLE

by

Alison Grant

with illustrations by

Mark Myers

GW00690298

NORTH DEVON MUSEUM TRUST
1991

Front Cover
Detail from The One and the Fifty Three. Watercolour by Mark Myers, 1990

Opposite
Sir Richard Grenville at age 29, from a portrait dated 1571, by an unknown artist

First published 1991 by North Devon Museum Trust

Copyright 1991 Alison Grant

Illustrations Copyright 1991 Mark Myers

ISBN 0 9504018 3 8

Printed in Great Britain by Devon County Council
and North Devon District Council

CONTENTS

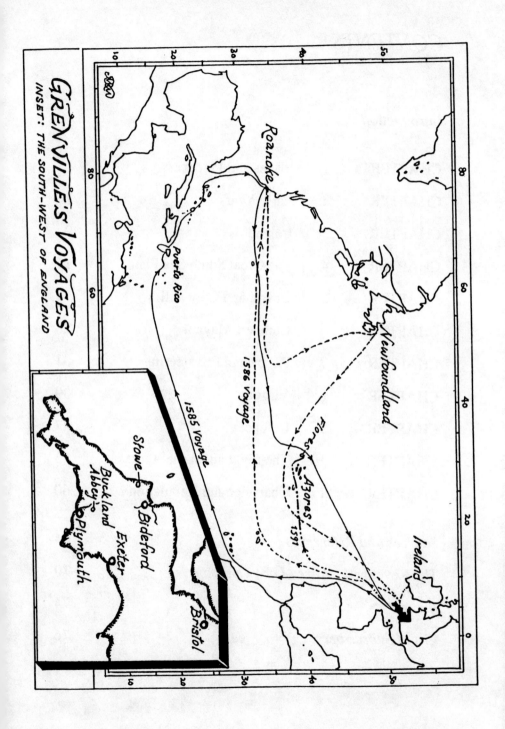

GRENVILLE'S VOYAGES

INSET: THE SOUTH-WEST OF ENGLAND

Roanoke

Puerto Rico

Newfoundland

Flores

Azores

1591

Ireland

1586 Voyage

1585 Voyage

Stowe
Buckland
Abbey
Bideford
Exeter
Plymouth
Bristol

INTRODUCTION

It is now 400 years since Sir Richard Grenville, in H.M.S. *Revenge*, took on a great Spanish fleet off Flores in the Azores. The tale will bear retelling, which is one reason for the publication of this book. It also seems a good time to attempt a brief account of Grenville's life, which has been lacking, perhaps because the ground is so thoroughly covered in the standard autobiography, A.L. Rowse's *Sir Richard Grenville of the Revenge*, first published in 1937. There is nothing to add to this well-researched, full-length work, but I believe there is room for a short study for general readers - and their children.

This book is not a work of original research, as there are no fresh sources to examine. I have drawn on Rowse, on some of his sources, and some more recent works, as can be seen from the list of references. I have chosen the subject because I live in Grenville country and specialise in local and maritime history. I am also a founder member and currently chairman of North Devon Museum Trust, which has its maritime museum at Appledore, with a view of the Pool there, where Grenville's ships must sometimes have anchored. The museum is mounting a quatercentenary exhibition on Sir Richard Grenville, and the book is published to co-incide with the occasion.

I am delighted that Mark Myers has agreed to illustrate this book. A noted marine artist, he lives in north Cornwall, which is also very much Grenville country. He has been a strong supporter of the North Devon Maritime Museum from the outset. I should also like to thank Pat Wiggett, the Museum Trust's honorary secretary, for typing the text.

This book is published by North Devon Museum Trust with help from North Devon Publications Group. All concerned with it have given their services free, and all profits from sales will go the the Museum Trust, which is a voluntary body set up to preserve and interpret the area's maritime and other heritage. It is also a registered charity.

Alison Grant   North Devon, 1991

The Grenville mansion at Stowe (after a contemporary painting). Although built after Sir Richard's time, it stood on the earlier site, commanding the same view over the Bristol Channel.

Mark Myers —

CHAPTER 1

Places and Predecessors

Richard Grenville was only eight years old in March 1551, when, by his grandfather's will, he became lord of the Cornish borough of Kilkhampton, and the nearby manor of Stowe with its 'mansion place', gardens, ponds, orchards, and park. He also inherited the manor of Bideford in north Devon, and, after his grandmother's death, Buckland Abbey near Plymouth.[1]

At Stowe, other than a farmhouse on the site of the old stables, nothing remains of Grenville's home, or even the one that succeeded it in the next century. The house was not far from the Bristol Channel, or Severn Sea as it was called. The coast here is inhospitable; high, rugged, lonely, and menacing, a graveyard for ships cast aground by nor-westerly gales at the foot of its rocky cliffs. It is not surprising that the first Grenvilles to settle here took little interest in the sea. Their house looked inland up the sheltered well-wooded valley to the good farming land on which the family fortunes were based.

Richard Grenville was descended from Norman adventurers who came to England soon after the conquest. It used to be thought that the west-country line was founded by Richard de Granville, who helped in the conquest of Glamorgan and founded Neath Abbey, then, it is said, went on crusade, returning at the ripe old age of 80 to settle on estates at Bideford in north Devon. It is more probable, however, that the family was descended from some relation of that doughty warrior. Bideford was another well-endowed manor, with the added benefit of a navigable river, and as one of their descendants said, 'the Grenvilles usually took the sea' there. By 1202 when a Sir Richard de Grenville paid 'ten marks of silver and one palfrey and one gold ring' to confirm his title to lands at Kilkhampton and Bideford, the family was firmly established in the west country.[2]

The Grenvilles were not well-known outside their own area, but they did occasionally produce a man of national importance, like William de Grenville, who became Lord Chancellor and Archbishop of York in the reign of Edward I. The family estates went to his elder brother, another Richard, who granted a charter to the town of Bideford, in exchange for a payment of four marks of silver (£2.66). He assured himself a regular income by keeping the profits from his

'Monday market', making the townspeople pay annual rents for the liberties he granted, and fining them if they failed to attend his monthly court. He thus linked his family's fortunes to those of the port, which was growing rich on the export of woollen cloth to France and Spain in exchange for wine and other goods.[3] In 1301 this same Richard de Grenville, questioned on his right to hold three annual fairs in Kilkhampton, declared that they and his market there had been held 'from time immemorial'.[4] Early Grenvilles were obviously successful lords of the manor and good businessmen, and the two market centres they established enhanced their own status and income, and benefited local people.

Over the next two centuries the Grenvilles managed to consolidate their lands and keep out of serious trouble. Thomas Grenville, who succeeded to the estates in 1483, nearly threw all this away by taking part in a Cornish plot to overthrow Richard III, but two years later, after the battle of Bosworth, he found himself on the winning side after all. He received a pardon, some minor favours, and a knighthood from Henry VII. He increased his family's importance by carefully arranged marriages, and as he had ten children, some of whom married more than once, the Grenvilles were amongst the best-related families in the west. Sir Thomas himself married into the Gilbert family of Compton in south Devon, and one of his daughters married a Raleigh. Thus, in due course, Richard Grenville could call both Humphrey Gilbert and Walter Raleigh, 'cousin'. Sir Thomas's numerous descendants spread the marriage net even wider, and eventually there was scarcely a gentleman in Devon and Cornwall who could not claim kinship with the Grenvilles. He died in 1513, four years after Henry VIII's accession, having done his duty by the Tudor monarchy as a JP, and taken his turn as Sheriff of Cornwall. His magnificently carved tomb still adorns the parish church at Bideford.

Sir Thomas's son, Sir Roger, inherited almost 1900 acres of land in Devon and Cornwall, together with 44 'messuages', the majority of them probably farmsteads. The capital value of his property must have been considerable, for his annual rents were assessed at of £60, a comfortable sum in those days. He enjoyed them for only a short time as he died in 1523, and was succeeded by his son, Sir Richard, often known as 'the elder' to distinguish him from his more famous grandson. This Sir Richard was later appointed Marshal of Calais, but fortunately for him, returned home just as the dissolution of the monasteries made much land available to gentry who supported the crown. Not slow to seek his share, Grenville wrote to Thomas Cromwell, Henry VIII's minister, asking for a royal gift of land, or at least the chance to buy at a bargain price, but apparently he was not high enough in the king's favour to obtain either. There were estates on the market, however, and he acquired Buckland Abbey in 1541, at a cost of £233. 3s 4d.[5] Soon afterwards he added other monastic lands in both

The Monument to Sir Thomas Grenville, Sir Richard's great-great-grandfather, in the Parish Church at Bideford.

Devon and Cornwall to his estateAs well as far reaching religious and social changes, the sixteenth century saw the growth of a new spirit among the English gentry as geographical discoveries opened up the known world and Renaissance arts and scholarship broadened intellectual horizons. The elder Sir Richard Grenville was both a man of action and a poet, although only two poems can certainly be ascribed to him. In the first, he wrote in martial mood, 'In Praise of Sea-faring Men in Hopes of Good Fortune'

> Who seeks the way to win renown,
> Or flies with wings of high desire...
> Who seeks to wear the laurel crown,
> Or hath the mind that would aspire;
> Tell him his native soil eschew
> Tell him go range and seek anew.

Following his own advice, Sir Richard had ventured abroad, if only as far as Calais, where he achieved at least a little renown. His other poem speaks for a seafarer, who, weary of travel, was content to

> ...leave the seas with their annoy,
> At home at last to live in joy.

Sir Richard's own last years at home were neither easy nor joyful. In 1549 he was caught up in the Cornish insurrection, known as the Prayer Book Rebellion, when he tried to hold Trematon Castle for the young king, Edward VI. It is said that he was tricked into going out to parley, whereupon the rebels, according to the account of the Cornish antiquary, Richard Carew, 'laid hold of his aged unwieldy body and threatened to leave it lifeless'. They went on to sack the castle, where the 'gentlewomen... were stripped from their apparel to their very smocks, and some of their fingers broken to pluck away their rings.'[6] Sir Richard and his wife died within a month of each other in 1550. It has been said that these hardships, and a period of imprisonment in Launceston Castle, also endured during the rebellion, hastened their death.

Whether or not they were familiar with his poems, the elder Sir Richard Grenville's son and grandson, may have been influenced by his interest in venturing abroad, for both sought their fortunes at sea. According to Carew, Sir Richard's 'martial employments... encouraged his son Roger the more hardily to hazard, and the more willingly to resign his life...'[7] By 1545, Roger Grenville had risen to be captain of the great Tudor warship, *Mary Rose*. On 19 July that year, during a war with France, he and his Vice-Admiral, Sir George Carew, a fellow west-countryman, were on board her at Portsmouth, when enemy ships were sighted. King Henry VIII was one of the horrified spectators as the great ship heeled over while getting under way, causing water to pour in through her open gunports and capsize her, sending five hundred or more men to the bottom.[8] Her captain was not among the handful of survivors, so old Sir Richard was left to mourn the death of his son, and make what provision he could, in the last few years of his life, for the infant grandson who was now heir to all his estates and ambitions.

Opposite

The Mary Rose *capsizing at Spithead, 19 July 1545. Her Captain, Roger Grenville, and some 500 men 'drowned like ratten' in this famous disaster.*

NORTH

WEST

Tavistock

Tavy river

Newbridg

Morel·ham

White·church

Horse bridg

Cuttel

Ralstoke

Dunmor bridge

Bockland

Sr Fr. Drake

Tynworkes

Rouber beacon

Rouber downe

Halton Roufe

Clifton Arundell

Serre

Cargreen

Lande y'pe

Brokan crosse

Bykel

Skirrele howe

Greatt crosse

Worle

Coppelstone

Hendstill

Tamerton

Saltash

Saltash passage

John to woods

Tre·mauton castell

St Stevv

Sr Bodolfe

Antony passage

MRM

The Tamar Valley above Saltash, after a Tudor map, c. 1590, in the British Museum. 'Clifton Arundell', where Grenville is thought to have spent much of his childhood, is the fourth house from the top on the left hand bank of the Tamar.

CHAPTER 2

Early Years

Richard Grenville was brought up by his mother, Thomasine, who soon married again. Her second husband was Thomas Arundell, a Cornish gentleman. The elder Richard Grenville sold him a monastic estate at Clifton on the Tamar, a few miles north of Saltash, and it is likely that young Richard spent much of his childhood there. It was not usual for the sons of gentry to go to school, so he was probably tutored at home, with his Arundell half-brothers. Most teachers were in holy orders, and those appointed for Richard Grenville would have been Protestants, for his grandfather had renounced the Pope, whom he called the 'devilish Bishop of Rome', and embraced the new religion. His monastic lands also gave him and many other west-country gentlemen an economic stake in the Reformation. Grenville was still a child when the Catholic, Mary I, came to the throne, but would have known some of the western men, who, strongly against her marriage to Philip II of Spain, were involved in conspiracies against the crown. Their leaders had to flee the country, but sympathy with them grew as Protestants who would not conform were burnt at the stake. Whether through the influence of tutors, family, other west-country gentry, or convictions personally acquired, Richard Grenville never wavered in his loyalty to the Protestant religion and opposition to Catholic Spain.

In spite of the troubled times, Grenville acquired enough book-learning to fit him for the status and duties of a gentleman, and perhaps a little more, for he was later to show himself capable in the acquisition and management of land, and well able to plan and write about projects in which he had an interest. There is no record that he went to university, but he did attend one of the Inns of Court, which was another way to set the seal on a gentleman's education. He began his studies at the Inner Temple in 1559, the first year of the reign of Elizabeth I. The legal training he received there probably served him well, and by bringing him to live in London for a while, rounded out his education.

Like most students, Grenville had his group of friends, mainly young bloods like himself, with retainers and hangers-on. Whether he got into bad company, or, with his powers of leadership, was bad company for others, he was involved in a serious fight with another such group in 1562, while still in London. Swords were drawn, and Grenville mortally wounded an opponent. He and a companion then fled, whereupon they were declared outlaws, liable to forfeit all their goods.

They were discovered and possibly imprisoned for a day or two, but were quickly brought to court, where Grenville was pardoned, possibly because he was still a minor. Tudor society tolerated, even tacitly encouraged such affrays, for every gentleman carried a sword, and had been trained to use it, and 'honour' was frequently satisfied by drawing blood. Young gentlemen not infrequently acted as Grenville had, and heirs to large estates could expect to get off lightly. The incident reveals a hot-blooded young man 'quick on the draw', and carried away by the passion of the moment and the will to win. Richard Grenville's character, it seems, was already formed.

Grenville came of age in 1563, and for a time occupied himself with the administration of the estates that were now his to control. He settled down for a while, and married the 'girl next door', Mary St Leger, whose father, Sir John, possessed lands at Annery near Bideford. Marriage, home, and family, however, were not enough for a spirited young man, when wars abroad were providing opportunities for action and renown. No doubt Grenville, at this time, agreed with the sentiments expressed by his grandfather in his martial poem many years earlier

> Wherefore who list to stay at home,
> To purchase fame I will go roam.

In 1566, Richard Grenville, with a group of friends and relations from the Devon gentry, went on 'crusade' against the Sultan, Solyman the Magnificent, who had invaded Hungary. The Holy Roman Emperor, Maximilian II, was glad to welcome 'gentlemen out of all parts of Europe', Catholics and Protestant alike, to help him turn back the Turks before they reached his capital, Vienna. For Grenville the campaign was short, for peace was signed not long after his arrival in Hungary. No details of any actions survive, although Richard Carew, the Cornish antiquary, writing of Grenville's career, mentioned his part 'against the Grand Turk, for which his name is recorded by sundry foreign writers'.[1] Those writers' accounts, if they ever existed, have been lost, like most other records of Grenville's early life. By 1568 he was home, and seeking adventure in some other sphere. He found it in Ireland.

CHAPTER 3

Ireland

Ireland, as the western frontier of Tudor rule, was, like the American West three hundred years later, a magnet for land-hungry adventurers and their armed followers. With the avowed aim of bringing the country under closer English control, the newcomers rode roughshod over both the native Irish and long-established Anglo-Irish settlers. Irish leaders retaliated with bloody uprisings, which were put down with great barbarity. Caught in the crossfire, peaceful residents and settlers lost their lives, or fled.

Sir Anthony St Leger, a cousin of Grenville's father-in-law, was one of the Tudors' most effective Lord Deputies in Ireland. In 1541, after fierce campaigning, he got Henry VIII declared King of Ireland, and head of the church there. By Elizabeth's reign, however, Roman Catholicism was re-established, and Irish chieftains often appealed to the Pope and the King of Spain for help against the English. They also fought amongst themselves, ravaging the country, and leaving the miserable survivors destitute.

In an attempt to solve these problems, Sir Henry Sidney, appointed Lord Deputy in 1565, sought to increase the number of English residents in Ireland. He found a willing ally in Sir Warham St Leger, Sir Anthony's son, who had inherited his father's Irish lands. Expecting to be appointed President of the province of Munster in southern Ireland, he invited Grenville to join him in building up an extensive 'colony' there. The two men planned to exploit the timber, monopolize fishing off the south coast, and bring out English settlers to cultivate the land.[1]

Grenville was well-placed for an Irish venture, with his west-country estates from which to recruit settlers, and the port of Bideford to provide shipping. Encouraged by being appointed Sheriff of Cork, the centre of the enterprise, he sold some of his English lands so that he could acquire large estates in Ireland. He sent out a number of settlers, and setting sail himself with his wife and children, joined Sir Warham's wife in Cork, in June 1568. St Leger himself had returned to England for a time, and Sidney, the Lord Deputy, was also out of the country. Hearing rumours of unrest amongst the Irish, Grenville decided to go back to England for re-inforcements. He apparently did not realise that the

9

province was already on the brink of revolt, and failed to make proper provision for the safety of those he left behind. Within 24 hours of his departure 2,000 men were up in arms, and Grenville's family and Lady St Leger were under siege in Cork.

The rebels were led by a member of the powerful Desmond family, who had a prior claim to the land allotted to the new English settlers. They began by attacking manor houses and laying waste to the land. Lady St Leger wrote to her husband that many of her retainers had been killed, and all horses and supplies taken, although she had managed to send a boat to bring some of her followers to Cork. There the rebels were making the end of the siege conditional on the surrender of the Englishwomen, as Lady St Leger made plain at the end of her letter, in a heartfelt cry for help, 'Good my Lord, take pity on me; they say plainly that they will never leave the town of Cork till they have me and the Sheriff's wife'.

Grenville and St Leger did their best to get the government to send troops to relieve Cork, but it was six weeks before their wives were rescued. It had been a close-run thing. Humphrey Gilbert, who was in Ireland pursuing ambitious plans of his own, was appointed to 'pacify' Munster. He made sure that the Irish were taught the cost of rebellion

> I slew all those...that did... maintain any outlaws or traitors; and after my first summoning of any castle or fort, if they would not presently yield it, I would not afterwards take it as their gift, but won it perforce, how many lives soever it cost, putting man, woman and child of them to the sword.[2]

Grenville returned to Munster with St Leger to help subjugate the rebels and restore order by the same methods, which they justified as revenge, for their wives had been in serious danger, and many of their tenants, servants and labourers had had their throats cut. By humanitarian standards they acted with appalling cruelty, but like Gilbert, who received a knighthood for his services in Ireland, they did not accept Irish claims to the land, and saw the savage punishment of rebels as a duty to the crown. They were not the only Elizabethan 'heroes' to put the Irish to the sword; Drake, for example, helped to annihilate a whole community in 1575, and Raleigh another in 1580.[3] All could justify their actions by the laws of England, and also by accepted laws of war, which allowed the slaughter of those who gave comfort to rebels, and all inhabitants of towns or castles which refused to yield to a besieging army. Shakespeare's audiences understood this when they heard Henry V call upon the governor of Harfleur to surrender, with chilling words

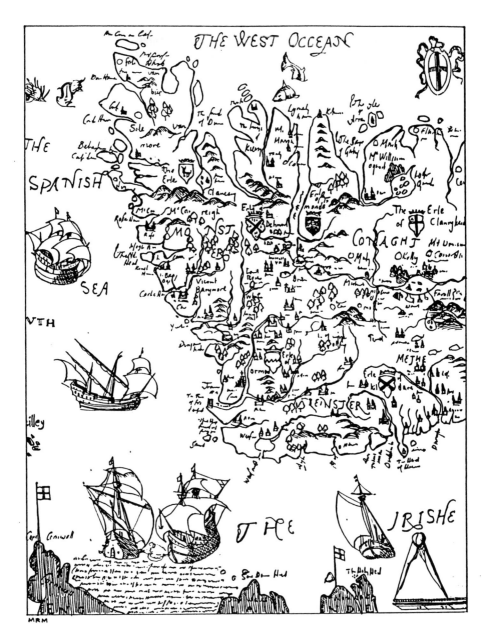

Southern Ireland from a map of 1567 by John Goghe. North is to the right, and Cork Harbour appears half way down the coast to the left, opposite the word 'Sea'. Cornwall is shown at the bottom left.

11

If not, why in a moment look to see
The blind and bloody soldier with foul hand
Defile the locks of your still-shrieking daughters;
Your fathers taken by the silver beards,
And their most reverend heads dash'd to the walls;
Your naked infants spitted upon spikes,
While the mad mothers with their howls confused
Do break the clouds...

The same threats were not only made, but carried out in Tudor Ireland.

In a short time Munster was laid waste, and the Irish leaders fled to the far west, whence they would emerge to fight another day. St Leger, who had failed to secure the Presidency of Munster, decided to abandon his plans, and return to England. Grenville had no choice but to follow. He had seen plenty of action, but had lost money and possessions, and was lucky to be able to bring his family home unharmed.

*   *   *   *   *   *

Although these early plans of Grenville's failed, he continued to take an interest in Irish affairs. After many outbreaks of savage fighting, the Irish Earl of Desmond was killed in 1583, and the government returned to the policy of planting Munster with English settlers, although there was a long delay while the land was surveyed and various claims were dealt with. Among those who responded to an appeal made to the gentlemen of the west was Sir Walter Raleigh, who began to settle English families on a large estate near Waterford. Meanwhile Sir Warham St Leger returned to the lands he had claimed many years before, drawing in Grenville once again as his partner.

There was a limit of 12,000 acres on estates granted at this time, but Grenville soon had twice as much, for he bought up a neighbour's property. By 1589 he had sent out about 100 settlers, but although a good many of his relations went out as lords of newly-acquired manors, there were not nearly enough farmers and labourers to cultivate the vast estates. Grenville, who also sent out some horses and farm stock, soon went to Ireland to see the situation for himself. Finding that he needed more tenants, he proposed in a memorandum that the Irish should have the right to lease land, and that burdensome dues imposed on them should be replaced with fairer taxes. This showed not only good business sense on his part, but also some statesmanship, for he pointed out that, freed from bondage, the Irish would 'become more obedient to her majesty'. If and when they strayed from that obedience, Grenville would no doubt have been ready to put them to the sword as before, but it is to his credit that he wanted to make a fresh and peaceful start.

Unlike many other English proprietors, who were absentee landlords, Grenville was prepared to live in Ireland for some years, and began building a house in the ruins of Gilly Abbey near Cork. He spent much of the year 1590 in Ireland improving his estates, intending to settle them on his second son, John. The next year, however, his work there was cut short by the queen's summons to sail with the fleet on the voyage from which, as it turned out, he did not return. It was said that he spent £8,000 on his ventures in Ireland, impoverishing his English estates in the process. John Grenville lost several legal and political struggles over the Irish lands he inherited, and three years after his own early death in 1595, another savage rebellion destroyed most of the English plantations in Munster.

Richard Grenville's Irish ventures had been a gamble. The prize he sought was, as Raleigh put it, a 'princely patrimony' for his heirs. To an English gentleman with one or more younger sons, the acquisition of cheap land was a great temptation. Grenville either did not realise the instability of the Irish situation at the time, or chose to take the risks involved. Characteristically he played for high stakes - and lost.

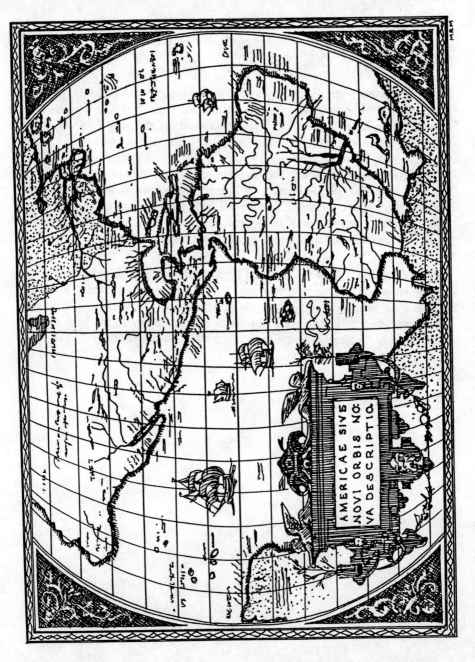

The South Seas and the Americas as known in 1570 (after a map in Ortelius's Theatrum Orbis Terrarum).

14

CHAPTER 4

The Great South Sea Plan

Richard Grenville, was not, like his great contemporary, Francis Drake, brought up to sail and navigate ships, but he was rich enough to buy and equip them for an expedition of discovery, conquest, and settlement. Like many of his friends and relatives in the west country Grenville was ready to take to the sea, for only by sea could the new world be explored and exploited, and by sea lay the most likely road to fame and fortune.

In 1574, Grenville petitioned the Queen for permission to lead an expedition to discover 'lands beyond the Equinoctial', i.e. south of the Equator, arguing that as Portugal and Spain had attained the eastern and western parts of the 'newefound world', and the French the north, the south had been 'by God's providence lefte for Englonde'. He found nine men willing and able to join him as principals in the venture. Of one, Martyn Dare, nothing is known, but most of the rest were 'gentlemen in the west parts', including Grenville's half-brother, Alexander Arundell, and three cousins, Arthur Bassett, John Fitz, and Edmund Tremayne. Another was a neighbour, Piers Edgecombe, whose estates overlooked Plymouth Sound not far from Buckland Abbey, which Grenville was rebuilding at the time. There were two merchants, Dominic Chester of Bristol, and William Hawkins of Plymouth, brother of the better known Sir John. The other man named was Thomas Digges, not a west-countryman, but married to a daughter of Sir Warham St Leger, and therefore one of Grenville's circle. He was a mathematician and geographer, whose skills would be needed 'to make plattes [maps] of every bay, road[stead], port or channel' discovered.

Grenville argued the case for his intended voyage in a lengthy paper which showed considerable knowledge of what might be involved. 'The matter itself which is offered to be attempted' consisted of discovery, trade and settlement 'of all or any Lands, Islands and Countries southward beyond the Equinoctial ... not already possessed...by any Christian Prince in Europe...'. He proposed to establish his first settlement from the River Plate southwards, as a place that 'the Spaniards or Portugals have not already added to their possession.' He would then sail on through the Straits of Magellan to the South Sea (Pacific Ocean) and establish further settlements on unclaimed land or islands. To complete his voyage, he proposed to 'ascend from the Equinoctial' along the west coast of North America to look for the western end of the North West Passage.

Having outlined his plan, Grenville argued its feasibility, and listed the means to achieve it :

> Ships of our own, well prepared.

> The West Country lying the aptest of all parts of England for navigation southward

> Mariners and sailors to whom the passage almost thither is known.

> The good and welcome commodities that from England shall be carried to that people, who being in the temperature of England and other parts of Europe cannot but like well of cloth wherein we most abound and the transportation whereof is most necessary for our people at home.

Here Grenville spoke like a good west-countryman, interested in shipping and the cloth trade, but in the next section on commodities to be brought home, the voice of the adventurer can be heard, with a reason more likely to appeal to Elizabeth I.

> The likelihood of bringing in great treasure of gold, silver and pearl into this realm from those countries as other Princes have out of the like regions.

The queen gave her consent to the plan, with a proviso that Grenville should first render some assistance to the Earl of Essex, who was engaged in a war of attrition with Irish rebels. As Deputy Lord Lieutenant of Cornwall, Grenville was expected to raise soldiers and see to their transport to Ireland. This he did with 'forwardness, diligence and good conformity to her Majesty's service', but afterwards it was too late in the season to embark on the voyage which he and his associates had planned for the summer of 1574. Preparations had gone ahead, watched closely by foreign spies. A Spanish agent wrote

> ...they ...assert that they are going to the straits of M.[Magellan], their fleet being increased by three sail, making ten ships in all, amongst which is the *Castle of Comfort,* a celebrated ship of 240 tons, the largest of them. The fleet is very well fitted and found, and will carry 1,500 men, soldiers and sailors, 500 of them being gentlemen. The real design is not known, as there are so many

plans afoot, but, as they are going in this guise, they probably mean to sack some of the islands and lie in wait for the ships from the Indies and other merchantmen. They say they are taking with them a store hulk of 600 tons with provisions, but I believe it is more likely to carry their plunder than to take stores. They sail this month...

It was unfortunate for Grenville that Philip II's spy-system was so efficient, for the letter, written in May 1574, gave early-enough warning of his intentions for complaints made in high places to take effect before the expedition could put to sea. The queen was trying to improve relations with Philip at this time, so, in spite of Grenville's protests that he would keep clear of Spanish settlements and 'take nothing from them that they have or claim to have', she revoked the licence she had issued for the voyage.

Grenville was never to undertake his great expedition to the south, yet his intended voyage sounds familiar, for leaving aside the settlements, it was the one undertaken by Drake in 1577, when Anglo-Spanish relations were once again strained, and the queen in an anti-Spanish mood. By that time Grenville's ideas were well known to most west-country seamen and promoters, and there is no doubt that Drake drew upon them. Grenville could only play the spectator while the other took his chance and won the glory. There is, of course, nothing to say that Grenville would have succeeded had he set out; Drake himself had enough trouble, not least over what he called 'the stomaching between the gentlemen and the sailors', which was only settled with strict disciplinary measures and the execution of Thomas Doughty.[1] Grenville proposed to take a large number of gentlemen on his expedition, so similar troubles might well have arisen. There is no point in speculating on how he would have dealt with such a situation, for fate - in the person of the queen of England - had willed that Grenville was not to be the first Englishman to lead an expedition to the Pacific, nor the *Castle of Comfort* the first English ship to circumnavigate the globe.

Mark Myers

CHAPTER 5

Devon and Cornwall

Whether he returned home fulfilled or frustrated, Richard Grenville had a choice of houses. He must have lived at Stowe for a while after his marriage, for an infant son, Roger, was buried at Kilkhampton in 1565. Bideford served well for his Irish ventures and later expeditions by sea, and when in London he used a riverside house at Southwark, formerly Sir Warham St Leger's. After the failure of his South Sea plans, he gave this up, and returned to the west country, to complete the conversion of Buckland Abbey to a great country house.

Grenville's 'mansion place' at Bideford, Place House as the locals called it, was where the Town Hall stands today.[1] There was no more convenient site in the town, for Grenville's predecessors as lords of the manor had built their house on the town boundary of their demesne, beside the church, and opposite the bridge. Often considered Bideford's glory, this bridge played an important part in the town's growth and prosperity. Six hundred and seventy seven foot long, with 24 arches, it was a remarkable achievement for its day.

Tudor Bideford. This reconstruction looks upriver from East the Water, showing Bideford Bridge, St. Mary's Church, the Manor House, and Quay.

At the time of Grenville's earlier Irish expedition, the town's fortunes were at a low ebb. There were complaints about the expense of maintaining the bridge, and it was said that 'it (Bideford) is greatly impoverished and standeth full of people...' Like other towns at the time, Bideford sought to shake off feudal restrictions and run its own affairs, claiming that 'for want of such liberties and privileges which other antient boroughs have..., the said village of Bedyford is made to decline into poverty.' Grenville, who had found Bideford a useful port, wisely decided to join the merchants, rather than obstruct them, and the alliance thus created served Bideford well. The townsmen agreed to confirm a number of Grenville's rights, and in return he secured a charter from Elizabeth I in 1574. This raised Bideford to the status of a corporation with a mayor, five aldermen, seven capital burgesses (councillors), and its own JP chosen annually from the aldermen. John Salterne, a merchant, became the first mayor, and Grenville himself served as one of the aldermen. The charter also confirmed the market and three annual fairs, and provided a sound basis for Bideford's economic progress. Grenville's Irish connections had a similar effect, for the Bideford

19

Grenville's Pier at Boscastle, built in 1584 and still in use.

men he took out as settlers, and the sailors who manned his ships began to forge links which played an important part in the expansion of the town's Irish trade in the next century.

Grenville's privateering and other shipping ventures also contributed to Bideford's prosperity, and he spent a good deal of time there preparing expeditions to Virginia in the 1580s (chapter 8). On 27 March 1588, an American Indian, a 'Wynganditoian', whom he had brought back with him from an earlier voyage, was baptised in the parish church of St Mary. There is no description of the ceremony, nor is it known whether the people of Bideford turned out to gaze, or whether they were as used to this stranger in their midst as to the doings of their Lord of the Manor. Grenville may have intended to take the Indian, who had been given the name Raleigh, back to his homeland as guide and interpreter on the expedition that was almost ready to sail, but in the event it did not set out, and Sir Walter's namesake died and was buried in Bideford the next year. [2]

Although Bideford was the port for many of Grenville's own expeditions, he realised the need for harbours of refuge and places of trade along the rocky north coasts of Cornwall and Devon. The sale of corn was important to rural areas, but to prevent shortages its export had to be locally controlled. In 1582-3, Grenville issued licences for shipping considerable quantities out of Cornwall, which may have drawn his attention to the need for harbour improvement. The next year, to the potential benefit of his own tenant-farmers as well as neighbouring landowners, he undertook the rebuilding of the quay and pier at Boscastle. The townspeople declared the work, done under his personal direction, 'most like for ever to continue', which was not mere flattery, for, with necessary repairs, it has withstood for 400 years the tides that rip and swirl in and out of that narrow inlet.

Grenville was soon afterwards asked to advise on new harbour works at Dover. He consulted the master of the works at Boscastle before giving his opinion, and sent a sketch-plan drawn by himself, together with advice on materials and methods of building. His fellow-commissioner for Dover was his Devon neighbour, George Cary, who was building the quay at Clovelly, and could well have discussed design and construction with Grenville, or been partly inspired by his work at Boscastle.[3] Labour for such schemes was probably recruited locally, but there were other sources. According to a letter sent to Spain early in 1588, 'Richard Grenville of Cornwall' had, more than two years earlier

> brought to England twenty-two Spaniards whom he treated as slaves, making them carry stones on their backs all day for some building operations of his, and chaining them up all night. Twenty of them have died or escaped...

What is significant here is not the harsh way in which Grenville treated his prisoners - after all, the Spaniards sent many of theirs to the galleys - but the fact that he used them for 'building operations'. Although the stones they carried could equally well have been used for houses, barns, or limekilns, the unfortunate Spaniards may have been constructing or repairing one of the small harbours along the coast of north Devon or Cornwall.

Grenville always maintained his interest in the affairs of his two counties. He was MP for the Cornish borough of Dunheved (Launceston) in all the parliaments called between 1563 and 84, and served on several committees. He consolidated his lands in the north of both counties. By the mid 1580s he owned, by inheritance or purchase, not only Stowe, Kilkhampton, and Bideford, but also estates or manors at Stratton and Morwenstow, Widemouth and Wolston, Swanacott, Week St Mary, Littleham and Landcross. He had also become Lord of Lundy Island when his father-in-law, Sir John St Leger, mortgaged it to him for £800 which was not repaid.[5] For a time in the 1570s, however, he turned his attention southwards, and, favouring Plymouth as a base for maritime enterprise, decided to make his headquarters at Buckland Abbey.

The Cistercian Abbey of Buckland had been founded in 1273, by Amicia, Countess of Devon, who endowed it with 20,000 acres of land. Its estates were split up at the Dissolution, and the elder Richard Grenville obtained only 570 acres of arable and pasture land when he purchased the abbey in 1541. These, however, were a valuable addition to the estates he already possessed. His son, Roger, may have lived there for a while, but after his early death Buckland appears to have been left in the care of tenants or agents until Richard Grenville began to take an interest in it after his return from Ireland. Like other new owners of monastic property he wanted a mansion at the centre of his estates, but unlike most of them he did not make use of domestic buildings. In spite of formidable architectural problems, he decided to make his great house in the abbey church itself.

The exterior of Buckland Abbey still bear the scars of Grenville's alterations. The cloisters and other monastic buildings on the north side of the church were demolished, and marks on the sides of the tower show where the transepts were torn down. The line of the medieval nave roof, which was removed and replaced with a lower one, can also still be seen. Chimneys show where fireplaces were inserted, and Grenville added a new kitchen wing at right angles to the original structure. Other alterations have further changed the look of the abbey over the years, but in spite of additions and subtractions, the centre of the house still resembles a medieval church .

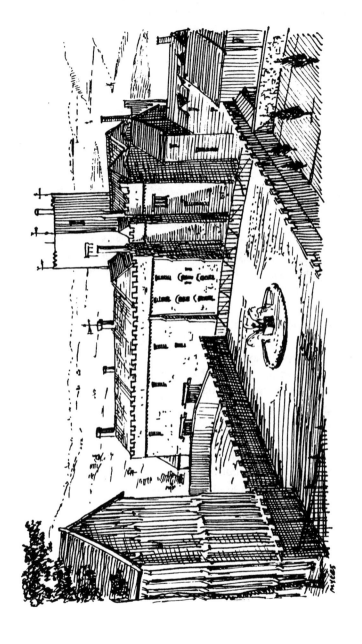

Buckland Abbey (after the engraving by S. and N. Buck, 1734). This early view includes the Tithe Barn on the left and, running to the left from the tower, the east wing built by Grenville.

Buckland Abbey is still essentially a sixteenth-century mansion, with much of the interior as Grenville left it. Only the occasional remains of medieval stonework 'outcrop' here and there to bear witness to the original use of the building. Living quarters were created inside the long, narrow nave by inserting two new upper floors, constructing staircases and partitioning off rooms, landings, and passages. Huge fireplaces dominate the kitchen, but the most impressive room is the Great Hall, built into the crossing below the tower, at the very centre of the old church. The remarkable plaster ceiling with interlaced designs, is coved above the fireplace where four large figures of satyrs seem to support it. The well-proportioned fireplace has a strong granite arch, surmounted with more plasterwork decoration, and figures representing Justice, Temperance, Prudence, and Fortitude. It bears the date 1576, which is thought to be the year the work was finished. Above the fine wood panelling of the west wall is a plaster frieze depicting knights who have turned their war-horses loose, and hung up their shields on trees, while they sit brooding on mortality, surrounded by symbolic skulls.[6] This kind of subject was common at the time, and there is no evidence that Grenville commissioned it when he returned to Buckland in melancholy mood after the failure of his cherished plans. Again, there is no evidence that he did not!

Building this country house must have given Grenville pleasure and pride, but even allowing for the use of timber and other materials from his estates, and the re-use of stone from demolished buildings, the work would not have been cheap. Although he had sold off the ships he had bought and fitted out for his abortive expedition, he must have suffered considerable financial losses which he now sought to recoup. He had already sold some of the abbey lands; did he really need a house near Plymouth now he could see no prospect of leading an expedition by sea? In any case he had Bideford, should the opportunity ever arise. In the newly-restored Buckland Abbey he had an asset of great value, if a suitably rich man wished to acquire it. As it happened, one did, and Grenville now had to choose between retaining his status symbol, and making good his losses. It is perhaps surprising that a man as proud as Grenville should have chosen to sell, especially as the would-be purchaser was the very man who had stolen his thunder. Grenville, however, with his usual business sense, swallowed his pride and sold his great house to none other than Francis Drake.

Grenville did not openly state resentment of Drake's success in the voyage he had wished to undertake himself, but it would have been surprising if he felt none. It is not true, however, as has frequently been stated, that rivalry between the two men prevented direct contact over the sale of Buckland, and that Drake secured the property by subterfuge, getting two other men to buy it then sell it to him. It is now evident that they, John Hele and Christopher Harris, simply acted as attorneys in the matter. In 1580, when the business was opened, Grenville may still have been somewhat unwilling to sell the house, and Drake, perhaps uncertain of how long he could maintain his newly acquired status, not ready to purchase outright. Grenville, however, needed ready money, and using Buckland as security, mortgaged the property for three years for £3400 to Hele and Harris who were acting on behalf of Drake. Unusually, it was the lender rather than the borrower who was entitled to pull out at the end of the time, should he wish to recover his money. Drake may have paid more for this option, for he certainly gave Grenville a handsome price. The elder Sir Richard had paid just over £400 for the property 40 years earlier, and even allowing for inflation and building work, his grandson obtained a good return. In the event Drake did not demand his money back, but kept the great house so conveniently situated for Plymouth, and there assumed the status of a country gentleman.[7]

Drake paid for Buckland Abbey from his share of the bullion from the *Nuestra Senora de la Concepcion*, otherwise known as the *Cacafuego*, the Spanish galleon he had captured on his voyage round the world. Deprived of the chance of such fabulous wealth himself, Richard Grenville thus, ironically, came by a portion of it.

The Grenville Arms

CHAPTER 6

Cuthbert Mayne

Richard Grenville, who had long served as a JP, was appointed Sheriff of Cornwall in 1577. His duties included keeping local Catholics in line, and tracking down secret congregations. Anti-Catholic feeling in England was increasing as Spain sought to crush the Protestant Netherlands, and the kings of France waged bitter wars against the Huguenots. At home the danger of plots and rebellions intensified after 1570 when the Pope excommunicated Elizabeth I. A few years later when English Catholic priests began to return from exile to re-convert the country to the Roman Church, they were regarded as foreign agents, and the government called on sheriffs to root out and make an example of them.

Cuthbert Mayne, by all accounts a mild, scholarly man, came from Shirwell in north Devon, where he was baptised in 1544. He was much the same age as Grenville, so both grew up in a period of great religious change. Mayne came from a fairly humble farming family, but an uncle sent him to the grammar school at nearby Barnstaple, which turned out some outstanding scholars in the sixteenth century, including John Jewell, bishop of Salisbury and apologist for the Church of England, and his Catholic adversary, Thomas Harding. Like these two great intellectuals, Mayne went on to Oxford, where he graduated and became a priest. At this time he was a Protestant, but after much soul-searching, and under the influence of Catholic friends, he joined the Roman Church. He escaped arrest in 1570 by returning to the west country, then taking ship to France. There he was ordained, and studied at the college at Douai set up to train priests for the English mission.

Cuthbert Mayne landed in Cornwall in the early summer of 1576. Although it was 27 years since Cornishmen had rebelled against the Protestant prayer book, and threatened and imprisoned old Sir Richard Grenville and his wife, memories were long, and among some of the gentry and their tenants there was still sympathy for the old religion. Francis Tregian, the Catholic lord of the manor of Golden near Probus, took Mayne into his household ostensibly as steward, secretly as priest. Here, and in houses belonging to other Catholic gentlemen of the neighbourhood, Mayne taught, converted, preached, and celebrated Mass for twelve months. When the news leaked out Grenville took vigorous action, for not only was this his duty as sheriff, but he could scarcely have forgotten what had happened to his grandparents. In June 1577, with the consent of the Bishop of Exeter who was in Truro at the time, he went to Golden, accompanied by a number of JPs, and, it is said, over 100 armed men. He told Francis Tregian, who came out to meet him, that he was looking for a prisoner called Bourne, who had escaped from London. Tregian swore the man was not there, and tried to bar Grenville's way, declaring that his house was his castle, and asking if the sheriff had a warrant to search it. Grenville, with his hand upon his dagger, forced him to give way, shouting, 'I will make an entrance either by your death or mine!' He stormed in and hammered at the locked door to Mayne's room. Mayne, who had apparently not been warned in time, entered the room from the garden and opened the door. Grenville seized him, shouting, 'What art thou?' The priest replied, 'A man', whereupon Grenville grabbed him by his doublet, demanding to know if he had a coat of mail under it. He found instead a locket containing an *Agnus Dei*, a little wax medallion depicting the Lamb of God. In 1571 the English parliament had passed an act making the possession of Catholic symbols a crime, so Grenville seized it, calling Mayne a rebel and a traitor.

The search of the house at Golden produced more evidence against Mayne. His books, letters and papers were seized, and he and Tregian were arrested and taken to Truro to be interrogated by the Bishop. Tregian, a gentleman, was allowed home on bail of £1,000. Mayne was left to face threats and abuse, not least from Grenville, who took personal charge of him during the journey to Launceston, where he was to face trial at the next Assizes. According to one account, 'Grenville exhibited his captive as if he were some strange monster, fastening him each night to the bed posts to prevent an escape.' On arrival, Mayne was thrown in chains into the dungeon at Launceston Castle to await trial. He was indicted under six counts, the most serious being that he had obtained a copy of the pope's 'Jubilee' Bull of 1575, and had published it at Golden. Mayne's defence that the Bull had no importance after the end of the Holy Year in which it had been issued, did not save him, for the act of 1571 declared it high treason to bring in and publish such literature in England.

Grenville was present at Mayne's trial to give evidence that the *Agnus Dei* and other possessions had been seized by him during his search of Tregian's house. A Catholic account, written after the event, relates that the trial was conducted in a hectoring spirit, with the senior judge, Manwood, apparently abusing and jeering at the prisoner. Another judge expressed some reservations, but Manwood directed the jury to find the prisoner guilty. When they returned it seemed they were not all agreed, whereupon Grenville leapt up and harangued them violently. The judge, thus encouraged, brushed aside the objections, and pronounced sentence. Although Catholic witnesses and writers saw Grenville as the villain of the piece, there is little reason to doubt this story, given his previous attitude to Mayne. Jurors frequently hesitated to condemn a man to a terrible death, but a reprieve for Mayne would have represented failure for Grenville, so he would scarcely have hesitated to browbeat the jury into giving the verdict he sought. He had done his duty as sheriff, and having got his man, wanted him convicted to prevent the spread of Catholicism in the county.

Mayne listened with composure to the sentence

> ...you are... to be dragged to the Market Place of this town [Launceston], where you are to hang until you seem half dead. Then your members and your bowels are to be torn out and burnt before your face. When your head is cut off, your body is to be divided into four parts to be sent to four places fixed by the Queen's authority.

There were still doubts about the trial, so Mayne was again imprisoned in chains in Launceston Castle, while the Queen's Privy Council investigated the matter. Many of the members wanted sentence carried out as an example, and Grenville, who went to London to give evidence, brought back the order for Mayne's execution. The priest was promised life and liberty if he renounced his religion, but would not do so. He also refused to acknowledge the queen as head of the Church of England.

Richard Grenville was absent on some other business when Mayne was executed at Launceston on 30 November 1577. His place was taken by his deputy, his nephew, George Grenville, who showed the condemned man at least a little compassion. He refused to allow Mayne's head to be dashed against the cobbles during the drawing, and decreed that he should hang until he was dead, to spare him the pain of the grisliest parts of the punishment. Mayne's quarters were sent to Barnstaple, where he had been to school, and to Bodmin, Tregony and Wade-bridge in Cornwall, to be displayed at the entrance to each town, to teach people the consequences of disobeying the established order in church and state.

Mayne's arrest was the signal for searching out other Catholics in Cornwall, of whom there now appeared to be an alarming number. During Grenville's absence in London Cornish Justices listed a number of gentlemen suspected of Catholic sympathies. Soon after Mayne was taken, 31 people were arrested at Golden, a striking example of what one priest could achieve. All but one of the prisoners refused to conform, and endured persecution, fines, or terms of impris-onment. Tregian did not escape; he was kept in prison for over 20 years, and died in exile in Portugal.

Grenville has been condemned for hunting down Cuthbert Mayne, but his position should also be viewed in the light of his own times. The government could not take the chance of further missionary activity in Cornwall where there was still sympathy for Catholicism. Mayne, with nothing left to fear, had made the danger clear during his last examination by the Justices on the day before his death. Catholics, he said, would, if called upon, be ready to help any Catholic prince who might invade the country to restore it to the Church of Rome. This made Mayne a militant Catholic, a dangerous man, and a traitor in the eyes of the government of an embattled Protestant nation, with an excommunicated monarch who was fair game for any would-be Catholic assassin. It was against this background that Grenville went about his duty as Sheriff of Cornwall; at such a time he was not expected to be over-scrupulous about the manner in which he carried out his task.

Almost four hundred years after his death, Cuthbert Mayne, the first of the Catholic martyrs of Elizabeth's reign, was made a saint of the church for which he had died. His persecutor did not have such a long wait for recognition; for his loyal services to county and country Richard Grenville was knighted in October 1577.

Launceston from the South Gate (after a print by F.W.L. Stockwell, 1822). The Castle where Cuthbert Mayne was imprisoned looms over the Town; the Market Square where he was executed lies in its shadow, behind South Gate.

Spoils of War, 1589. The captured flyboat alongside Bideford Quay.

30

CHAPTER 7

Piracy and Privateering

...entered from the sea, a flyboat, John Davies, master;

for Richard Grenville

26	hh[?]* of oil
80	barrels of figs
300	peces* of figs
1,070	lbs of wax [1]

A vessel 'entered from the sea' was a prize, and this un-named flyboat had been captured and sent to Bideford by one of Grenville's ships. John Davies, the prize-master, had brought it in with a crew from the privateer, which carried extra men for the purpose. Unfortunately there is no detail of what pursuit, bloodshed, or even loss of life lay behind this entry made by the local controller of customs in his 'port book' for 1588-9. Flyboats, medium-sized cargo carriers, were developed and much used by the Dutch, so the prize may have been owned in the Protestant Netherlands.[2] Her cargo, however, could have come from Spain or Portugal, with which England was at war. Ships carrying cargo to or from enemy ports were reckoned fair game, for privateering voyages could yield enormous profits, and those who sent them out did not look too closely into what constituted a war, or who exactly were enemies. Some of Grenville's ships pursued and looted any vessels they met, including, on at least one occasion, an English one.

Customs dues came to about five per cent of the value of prize cargo, and the queen could also claim five per cent of any precious metals. Finally, after the Lord Admiral (who at this time was Lord Howard of Effingham) had had his 'perks' of ten per cent, the goods could be sold and the takings shared out. The 'adventurers', who had risked their money to fit out and victual the privateer usually retained two thirds for expenses and profit, while the crew received the

* The entry is not clear. It is most likely to be hh, meaning hogsheads, ie large barrels. A p(i)ece was also a kind of cask.

31

other third, and usually the right to pillage everything except actual cargo - passengers' possessions, for example. This division of spoil encouraged local gentry and merchants to finance voyages, and seamen to pursue and engage ships to increase their share of the plunder. The captured vessels would, if official procedure was followed, be 'condemned' in local Courts of Admiralty, then sold to increase the profit of the venture. Like other adventurers, Grenville added a number of prizes to his own fleet.

Grenville had been a shipowner at least since his first Irish venture. A correspondent writing from Cork in 1568, reported that the rebels were threatening to burn a 'tall ship of Sir Warham St Leger's and Mr Grenville's,' which was lying at anchor in the harbour. This may have been newly acquired, for she was 'very well appointed', as befitted the status of her owners. It is not known whether she was destroyed in the rebellion; if not, she may have been used to raid Irish shipping, as suggested by a correspondent in Ireland.[3] Her owners would have justified such attacks as an attempt to recoup their own losses. Reprisals were the official justification for privateering, and were 'legalised' by letters of marque issued by the crown - and sold by its servants - usually, but not invariably, in wartime. Without such licenses raids on shipping were acts of piracy.

Piracy in English waters was dealt with by local sheriffs and JPs, so Grenville was called upon more than once to enquire into the activities of renegade English captains off the coasts of Cornwall. Captain Piers of Padstow, for instance, no doubt deserved to be investigated; his mother was found hiding a 'great rug' which had been brought ashore, and the captain had armed followers, and some trifling amounts of gold and silver for which he could not easily account. Grenville's evidence probably helped to convict him when he was eventually taken; it could be said that it took one pirate to hang another.

Gentlemen pirates were seldom, if ever, hanged, for there was literally one law for the rich and another for the poor. In 1574, eight years before the investigation into Captain Piers's petty piracy, a Spanish agent had written of 'an English gentleman named Grenfield, a great pirate...' from which it may be assumed that Grenville had previously sent out raiding ships, or even led expeditions himself, although there is no evidence that he had seafaring experience at that time. The *Castle of Comfort*, which he had bought in partnership with William Hawkins for his projected South Sea voyage, was one of the largest and best armed English ships in the business. Soon after the expedition was called off, she captured the *Sauveur* of St Malo, claimed by her owners to be worth £15,000. Questioned in the Court of Admiralty in London, Grenville denied any part of the action, maintaining that just before the ship sailed, he and Hawkins had sold her to a French Protestant who had a Huguenot letter of marque, and so was entitled to take the Catholic St Malo vessel. He was forced to admit, however, that he and Hawkins had victualled and furnished the *Castle of Comfort,* and engaged a crew of Englishmen before the alleged sale took place. The verdict of this case does not survive, but the two west-countrymen stuck to their unlikely story - and to the prize.

Shipowners and captains who attacked ships of other nations did not regard themselves as pirates, but justified their actions in several ways. They did not accept Spanish claims to all the land, treasure, and trade of the new world, so when attacked in Spanish waters, claimed provocation and loss, sometimes with good reason; in 1568, the Spanish governor of St Juan de Ulua in the Gulf of Mexico, promised safe conduct for a small fleet under John Hawkins, which had put into the harbour there for repairs. He broke his word, and in a surprise attack the Spaniards sank or crippled all but two of the English vessels, with great loss of life. The incident created lasting bitterness, and was used to justify later raids against Spanish ships and settlements, not only by Hawkins and Drake who had suffered personally, but by Englishmen in general. Such given reasons for raiding, however, were usually but a thin disguise for robbery with violence upon the high seas.

In 1585 Grenville, leading his first expedition to Virginia (Chapter 8), sailed to the Caribbean where he took two small Spanish vessels for his own use, seizing their cargoes, and holding the crews to ransom. As it was not wartime, this was an act of piracy, but later that year the uneasy peace between England and Spain finally broke down, so letters of marque became available to 'legalize' English privateering. Grenville, who greedily seized the chance for all-out pursuit of prizes over the next few years, anticipated his licence on the way home from Virginia, when

> he descried a tall ship of 400 tons or thereabouts, making the same course as he did; unto whom he gave chase and in a few hours by goodness of sail overtook, and by violence won, richly laden with sugar, hides, spices, and some quantity of gold, silver and pearls.

Another account, claiming that he boarded this prize 'with a boate made with boards of chests, which fell asunder, and sunke at the ship's side, as soon as ever he and his men were out of it' demonstrates the single-minded determination

Sir Richard's boarding party coming alongside the Santa Maria de San Vicente *in their improvised boat, 1585.*

with which Grenville pursued plunder. A Portuguese merchant taken prisoner in the action provided further detail, relating that Grenville first fired into the rigging to reduce the ship's speed, then pursued her, firing constantly and causing casualties, before a hole below the waterline forced her to lie to. Boarding with thirty armed men, Grenville quickly relieved the passengers of the keys to their boxes, breaking open those he could not unlock, in his haste to possess the gold, silver and pearls they contained. He then demanded the list of the ship's cargo, and had all valuables handed over. Not surprisingly he decided to stay on board himself, so sent half the Spaniards back to his own ship, from which he was later separated by a storm. He called at the Spanish island of Flores, and demanded stores by threatening to throw his prisoners overboard. After getting what he wanted, he freed them after having them searched again to see if they were carrying any valuables ashore.[4] The prisoner who wrote this account was obviously biased against Grenville, but there is nothing here which cannot be believed; successful privateers - or pirates - had to be ruthless and efficient, and this account shows that Grenville was both.

The prize was the *Santa Maria de San Vicente* a galleon of 400 or more tons, and in due course Grenville triumphantly sailed her into Plymouth himself. The pearls went to the queen, and the prize, worth £50,000 according to one account, probably paid for the voyage as well as helping to restore Grenville's fortunes. He returned to Virginia in 1586, searching ships *en route*, and sending home two Breton vessels and a Dutch ship that had Spanish goods on board. These seizures were not upheld by English courts, and Grenville's prize captains were ordered to make restitution of some of the goods. Whether they did so is doubtful, for while the cases dragged on, the Lord Admiral had accepted his tenths, and the captured ships were taken into Grenville's fleet of privateers. After leaving Virginia he continued the hunt for prizes on both sides of the Atlantic, even going back as far as Newfoundland for supplies, and delaying his return until he at last captured a rich Spanish frigate off the Azores. His return to Bideford was noted by Philip Wyot the town clerk of nearby Barnstaple;

> In December this year [1586] Sir Richard Greynfild came home bringing a prize with him, laden with sugar, ginger and hyds.[5]

The following few years were also profitable for Grenville who continued to send out privateers under captains as unscrupulous as himself. The names of Richard Willett, and Arthur and John Facy, all of Bideford and all employed by him, appear frequently in Admiralty Court records, and in one shameful episode, Arthur Facy and another captain, in two small ships, the *Brave* and the *Roe*, bound for Virginia in 1588, endangered the lives of the settlers on board in order to pursue and plunder every ship possible. The *Brave* was then boarded herself, and looted after a savage fight, which meant that she was unable to complete the voyage to Virginia. The *Roe* also turned back. In that year, in view of the expected arrival of the Spanish Armada, Grenville's larger vessels had been prevented from making the voyage to Virginia; they would probably have behaved no differently, but their size and armament would have given them

The departure of Grenville's fleet for Virginia from Plymouth, 1585.

more chance of success. Afterwards Grenville employed them for privateering, and in 1590 the *Galleon Dudley* sent in to Falmouth 'a Spaniard or Portugall laden with wollen cloath, oyles, wines and other merchandize'.

The onset of war thus brought good fortune to adventurers like Grenville and Raleigh, who were partners in many ventures at this time. Peacetime piracy could be adjudged reprehensible, but when the country was fighting for its freedom privateering was a patriotic act and successful crews as popular as war heroes in any age. Many coastal towns became noticeably richer, building new quays and houses as standards of living rose among all concerned with shipping. Most seamen, although their lives were at stake, sought prize money as a much-needed supplement to their miserable wages, and shared with the merchants and gentry who ventured capital the dream, and quite often the reality, of instant riches. The queen and many of her ministers personally supported privateering, and Grenville was no more rapacious in pursuit of plunder than Drake and many other Elizabethan seamen, famous or obscure. Most of their contemporaries backed them to the hilt, for the harder they hit the enemy the richer became all associated with them.

CHAPTER 8

Virginia

Sir Richard Grenville was over 40 before he set out on his first major expedition by sea. When the opportunity came at last, in 1585, he wrote that he was prepared to commit himself 'to the pleasure of God on the seas'.[1] He did not have to worry about lack of experience, for ship handling could be left to mariners, and it is unlikely that he saw any need to 'haul and draw' with them in the Drake tradition. Grenville's exploits by sea were an extension of his activities on land. Trained to bear arms and used to command, he led boarding parties, foraging expeditions and journeys into the unknown with aggression and great personal courage, but not always with cool judgement.

Many Elizabethan gentlemen who went to sea simply turned pirate or privateer, but others, while not neglecting opportunities for plunder, hoped to promote English trade and settlement in the new world - and add to their own wealth and status in the process. Grenville himself had planned to colonise lands south of the equator, and a few years later Humphrey Gilbert saw an opportunity in the vast unexplored lands of North America, and got a patent from the queen to settle Englishmen there in areas as yet unclaimed by Europeans. On Gilbert's first expedition in 1578 his half-brother, Walter Raleigh captained a ship which, like the others, was forced to turn back. By the time Gilbert had managed to equip a second expedition in 1583 Raleigh had risen so high in the queen's favour that she refused to part with him. Gilbert reached Newfoundland, which he claimed for the crown, but after various accidents left him with only two ships, he chose to return in the smaller one, the *Squirrel*, of only eight tons. Proclaiming that he was 'as neere to heaven by sea as by land', he was lost in an Atlantic storm.[2]

Gilbert's North American patent lapsed, but in 1584 the queen granted virtually the same rights to Raleigh. Some of Gilbert's other associates claimed rights in Newfoundland and the north, so Raleigh turned his attention farther south, where a colony might also provide a base for raids on Spanish shipping. The two ships he despatched to reconnoitre possible sites in 1584 returned with glowing reports of the nature and potential of the land, and 'brought home also two of the Savages being lustie men, whose names were Wanchese and Manteo'. Raleigh, recently knighted, named the area Virginia in honour of the queen, and began to fit out a full-scale expedition to take out the first settlers. Still detained at court, he gave its command to Grenville, who, 'from the love he bore unto Sir Walter

40

Raleigh, together with a disposition he had to attempt honourable actions worthy of honour, was willing to hazard himself in this voyage'. The expedition sailed from Plymouth in April 1585, Grenville's squadron

> consisting of seven sailes, to wit the *Tyger*, of the burden of seven score tunnes, a Flie-boat called the *Roebucke*, of the like burden, the *Lyon* of a hundred tunnes or thereabouts, the *Elizabeth* of fiftie tunnes, and the *Dorothie*, a small barke; whereunto were also adjoyned for speedy services, two small pinnesses.

One of the pinnaces was lost in a storm off Portugal, which also scattered the rest of the fleet. The *Tiger* went on alone, and after a remarkably fast passage reached the Caribbean less than a month after leaving Plymouth. Grenville made for a pre-arranged rendezvous at Puerto Rico where after some days he was joined by the *Elizabeth*. He had already set his men to fell trees to build a fort and a new pinnace. When the Spaniards refused to sell him provisions, he smartly captured two of their ships, which he added to his fleet. Taking the crews prisoner, he threatened to hang them if stores, cattle, and horses were not handed over.

Grenville soon got what he wanted, freed his prisoners, and set off for Hispaniola. The Spaniards here thought it prudent to welcome such strongly-armed ships and men. Courtesies were exchanged, and the English erected

> two banqueting houses covered with greene boughes, the one for the Gentlemen, the other for the servaunts, and a sumptuous banquet was brought in served by us all in plate, with the sound of trumpets, and consort musicke, wherewith the Spaniards were more than delighted.

Elizabethan gentlemen kept up ceremony, and those of Grenville's rank did not go to sea without musicians and services of silver plate! Next day the English

> played the merchants in bargaining with them' and secured 'horses, mares, kine, buls, goates, swine, sheepe, bull-hides, sugar, ginger, pearls, tabacco and such like commodities of the Iland.

Opposite

'The Arriual of the Englishemen in Virginia', after Theodore de Bry's engraving of a drawing by John White. Roanoke Island is left centre.

Having treated the Spaniards with both the iron hand and the velvet glove, and secured the necessary stock and provisions for the colony, Grenville began to make his way northwards along the coast of Florida, reaching the Outer Banks of what is now North Carolina towards the end of June. In a shallow inlet called Wococon by the Indians, the *Tiger* went aground and was pounded by heavy seas for two hours. She was eventually saved but the provisions she carried were much damaged, and she needed extensive repairs. Grenville, who had brought back the two Indians, now sent a message to Wanchese's chief at Roanoke Island some miles north, the most likely site for the colony. A party sent off to explore returned with the welcome news that the *Roebuck* and the *Dorothy* were in the vicinity, and another boat brought back two men from the *Lion*, which had been and gone, having landed them and about 30 others before going off to hunt for prizes farther north.

Grenville now decided to explore the country himself in his 'tilt boat', a wherry he had had shipped aboard the *Tiger* with such expeditions in mind. He was accompanied by John Arundell, his half-brother, and a party of about 60 gentlemen and mariners in the new pinnace and a couple of ships' boats. They explored Pamlico Sound between the mainland and Outer Banks, and when they went ashore John White, the Cornish-born artist and mapmaker who accompanied the expedition, made sketches of Indians and their villages. At most of these the party was 'well entertained ... of the Savages', but the expedition was marred by an incident at a village called Aquascogak where an Indian stole a silver cup, which probably belonged to Grenville himself. One of the boats was sent to demand its return, but when this was not forthcoming, the Englishmen 'burnt and spoyled their corne, and Towne, all the people being fled'. Grenville and his companions were happy enough to accept help and hospitality from the Indians, but saw them as pagan savages, not equals. The country had been claimed for the queen by virtue of her patent to Raleigh, and Grenville recognised no other jurisdiction. In his judgement, those who dared to steal and conceal the silver cup had to be taught a sharp lesson. In Virginia, as in Ireland, he apparently did not consider that such behaviour might rouse the natives against English settlers. On the other hand he was on the edge of the wilderness among warlike tribes, so he probably thought a show of strength justified. There was no bloodshed on this occasion, but the punishment inflicted was out of proportion to the loss.

On Roanoke Island, work began on the construction of a fort, and probably also a fortified enclosure to protect the rush-thatched 'cottages', the store, and other buildings. Grenville presumably had some part in choosing the site at the northern end of the island, at the head of the creek - unfortunately there was no deep harbour. He sailed for home on 25 August 1585, leaving 107 men on the

Their rype Corne

Their greene corne

Corne newly sprang

Their sitting at meate

The howse wherein the Tombe of their Herounds standeth

SECOTON

A Ceremony in their prayers w[i]th strange gestures and songs dansing abowte post carved on the topps lyke mens faces.

The Indian Village of Secoton on the mainland near the Roanoke Colony. Detail after a drawing by John White.

43

island, fewer than originally intended. This was probably due to the loss of provisions when the *Tiger* went aground, an accident which had other serious effects for the new colony, for the settlers had to depend on Indian help or live off the country while waiting for the arrival of ships with more stores.

Colonel Ralph Lane, leader of the soldiers on the expedition, was left in charge at Roanoke. He had secretly written home to complain of his commander's 'intolerable pride and insatiable ambition', so was pleased to see Grenville go. Quarrels were common on long expeditions, and Grenville was not the only leader to incur such resentment; in 1578 Drake had executed Thomas Doughty, whom he saw as a threat to his authority. Lane accused Grenville of intending to treat him in the same way, because he had offered 'advice in a public consultation'. Grenville, who was not a man to take criticism quietly, probably viewed this as an open challenge to his position, and felt he had the right to obedience, for the expedition could have come to grief had he failed to enforce discipline either on board ship or in unknown territory. Unlike Lane, who asked to be relieved of any future service under him, he appears to have borne no lasting resentment, for he left him in charge of the settlement. Although Grenville's overbearing manner and strong temper were resented by other subordinates besides Lane, he was a capable leader who 'performed the action directed, and took possession and peopled a new country, and stored it with cattle, fruits and plants'.[3] These considerable achievements, together with the capture of the *Santa Maria de San Vicente* on the homeward voyage, (Chapter 7) ensured that Raleigh asked him to lead the next expedition to Virginia.

Grenville, who had done well from the capture of the *Santa Maria*, probably invested more heavily in the new expedition than he had in the first. It is significant that he fitted it out at Bideford, his 'home' port, and the ships that departed thence are likely to have been at least partly owned by him. They had to cross the notorious Bideford (or Barnstaple) bar to get out to the Bristol Channel. Philip Wyot of Barnstaple wrote in the diary he kept,

> 16th April [1586] ...Sir Richard Greynvylle sailed over the barr with his flee boat and friget, but for want of sufficient water on the barr being neare upon neape, he left his ship. This Sir Richard Greynvylle pretended [intended] his going to Wyngandecora where he was last year'.[4]

Wyngandecora was the Indian name for the part of Virginia explored by Grenville in 1585.

The word ship often meant a vessel of some size, and Grenville may have fitted out one of the Spanish prizes he had taken the year before. Whatever the vessel, the incident caused delay, and the expedition did not leave until the end of April or early in May. On the voyage Grenville pursued prizes (Chapter 7), which further delayed the expedition and reduced available manpower, with serious consequences. He had no reason, however, to think that the settlers needed urgent relief, for he knew that Raleigh had already sent a small fast-sailing vessel, 'freighted with all manner of things in most plentiful manner for the supply and relief of his colony then remaining in Virginia'.

The colony in Virginia had not prospered. The Roanoke Indians had turned hostile, first denying supplies, then gathering in force with the intention of attacking the settlement. Lane took the offensive and attacked first, killing the chief and a number of his men. Thus danger was averted for a time, but fear remained. The settlers had sown some corn, but meanwhile were forced to live on roots and shellfish. Their morale became lower when no relief ship arrived in April as expected. It was not until early June that sails were sighted; neither Raleigh's ship, nor Grenville's but Drake's privateering fleet, homeward-bound from the 'Spanish Main'. He had intended to make contact with the Roanoke colony, but expected to find a better-established settlement, and did not know until his arrival that no supply ships had arrived. He could and did offer immediate relief, but did not have enough food to leave for a colony that had no idea when or even whether supplies might arrive. While Lane considered what to do, a storm drove some of Drake's vessels out to sea, and damaged others lying in the colony's inadequate harbour. Drake was in a hurry to depart, and seeing no certainty of future relief, Lane decided that the only way to save the settlers' lives was to sail with him. The colony was abandoned on 17 June 1586, 'and for feare they should be left behind they left all things confusedly, as if they had bene chased from there by a mighty army'. Thus, when the long-awaited ships arrived there was nothing to tell them what had happened to the settlers.

Raleigh's supply ship, which probably arrived within a few days of the evacuation, sailed off to search the coast, thus missing Grenville who at last turned up in mid-July. He too searched the surrounding country but heard no news of the settlers. In the end,

> unwilling to loose the possession of the Countrie which Englishmen had so long held; after good deliberation, hee determined to leave some men behinde to reteine possession of the Countrey; whereupon he landed fifteene men in the Ile of Roanoak, furnished plentifully with all manner of provision for two yeeres, and so departed for England.

45

Grenville, who took a 'Wynganditoian' to England, must have made contact with Indians on this expedition, and learnt that fighting had taken place, yet he left a small party with little chance of survival. He would not have wanted to deplete his own numbers further, for he intended to pursue prizes on the way home, and it is unlikely that many of his men were willing to stay behind and lose anticipated rewards. A larger force might have held the colony, but Grenville was more interested in ensuring that this voyage, like the first, would pay for itself, which it eventually did. No doubt this success was commended by Raleigh, who was no less interested in prizes and profit. It was the tiny garrison left on Roanoke that paid the price. According to an account given by Indians to the artist, John White, who returned to Virginia with settlers in 1587, some of the 15 men were killed in an Indian attack on the fort, and the survivors fled in a boat, perhaps only to suffer the same fate elsewhere, or be lost at sea. They were never heard of again.

Grenville did much to establish the first English settlement in the New World, but he also contributed to its failure. He shared Raleigh's genuine interest in colonisation, but with no government finance, expeditions had to be paid for by the promoters. Both men let privateering, which should have been only the means to an end, become an end in itself. When it became clear that Virginia was not, after all, very well-placed for a privateering base, even Raleigh became less enthusiastic, although his name was associated with several more voyages to Virginia. Grenville, as it turned out, did not return there.

CHAPTER 9

Defence

'Much afraid of a Spanish invasion', wrote Philip Wyot of Barnstaple in his diary in the summer of 1588.[1] In spite of rumours of foreign attack, the government was not prepared to spend much on royal ships let alone maintain a standing army, but expected Justices of the Peace and other officials to arrange local defence. Coastal towns and shipowners had to provide armed vessels and crews when called upon, while the local gentry were expected to repair coastal forts, and muster men to defend their shires.

In 1583, Grenville was appointed one of the commissioners for the coastal defences of Devon and Cornwall, a responsible job, for the south west could well have been the first landing place for invaders. He carried out his task conscientiously, showing considerable knowledge of surveying and fortification, for instance in the report on Tintagel he sent in at the end of the year. He was also 'much engaged in the musters' at this time. According to law, all the able men of a town or parish were obliged to form a militia or 'home guard', and turn out for training in the use of bows, bills, pikes, and hackbuts (harquebuses) - clumsy and somewhat unreliable firearms. These weapons, together with armour and horses, had to be provided or paid for by the better-off residents. Grenville organised the militia in north Cornwall, and his military experience enabled him to advise in other areas. He was present, for example at a muster in Barnstaple in February 1587, perhaps to help the young Earl of Bath, recently appointed Lord Lieutenant of Devon, a position involving responsibility for the militia of the county.[2]

Lords Lieutenant were usually noblemen, so anger was caused in aristocratic circles by the appointment of a commoner, Sir Walter Raleigh, to the Lieutenancy of Cornwall in 1585. Among commoners, Grenville, who had estates in the county and had for some time served as Deputy Lieutenant, had a better claim, but he was not the queen's favourite, so once again found himself serving his cousin. There is no record that he complained, for there seems to have been a genuine affection between the two men, and Raleigh later commended Grenville's loyalty and willingness in the queen's service.

The queen's service prevented Grenville leading Raleigh's next expedition to Virginia, which set out in 1587 with 150 settlers under John White as governor

Devon and Cornwall 'as they were to be fortified in 1588 against the Landing of any Enemy', after an engraving by John Pine. Tiny symbols denoting companies of local militiamen dot the coastline.

Instead he was detailed by the Privy Council to survey all 'places of descent' - possible enemy landing places - in Cornwall and Devon, and recommend measures to defend them. He also received orders to muster and inspect personally the militia of both counties, report on their equipment and training, and recommend improvements. In this he even took precedence of the Earl of Bath who was ordered to assist him. Grenville did his work as thoroughly as the Council had expected, and in June 1587 reported that Cornwall had 1600 trained men. It sounds a puny force to resist the armed might of Spain, but no doubt Sir Richard Grenville, himself captain of 300 Cornish militiamen, was ready to give any invaders a run for their money.

When Grenville had finished these duties, the Privy Council, according to reports leaked to the Spanish ambassador, discussed sending him to sea with reinforcements for Drake, who having 'singed the King of Spain's beard' at Cadiz, was still raiding the Spanish coast. According to the informer the Council feared, however, that Grenville 'would not serve Drake, and it was necessary to send some person who would not raise questions but would obey Drake unreservedly.' It sounds as if the King of Spain was well-informed on English plans, and the Privy Council on Grenville's reputation! There is no evidence that Grenville put to sea at all in 1587, but after June nothing is known of his activities for several months, so he could have been given some command, or gone privateering. If so he was back by the autumn, when he was appointed to a committee of 'noble and experienced captains' to report on the best means to counter the expected invasion. The 'mole' then informed the Spaniards that Grenville was being sent to Plymouth to prepare defences there.

Early in 1588 all men of fighting age - between 16 and 60 - were mustered, and by April Cornwall reported 5,776 able men, and Devon 10,000, although not all were equipped and trained. Grenville, having now finished the work given him by the Council, turned his attention elsewhere. John White had returned from Virginia with a list of the 'knowen and apparent lackes and needes' of the new settlers he had left there. A relief expedition was planned but events at home prevented it from sailing

> Sir Walter Raleigh ... promised that with all convenient speede he would prepare a good supply of shipping and men with sufficience of all thinges needefull which he intended, God willing, should be with them the Sommer following. Which pinnesse and fleete were accordingly prepared in the West countrey at Bidiforde under the chardge of Sir Richard Greenvil. This fleete being now in a

redinesse only staying but for a faire wind to put to Sea, at the same time there was spread throughout all England such report of the wonderfull preparation and invincible fleetes made by the King of Spaine joyned with the power of the Pope for the invading of England, that most of the ships of warre then in a readines in any haven in England were stayed for service at home: And Sir Richard Greenevil was personally commanded not to depart out of Cornewall. The voyage for Virginia by these meanes for this yere [was] thus disappointed...

Thus it was that Barnstaple's town clerk noted in his diary that 'five ships went over the bar to join Sir F.D. at P'mo.'[4] In spite of claims later made by Barnstaple, these vessels belonged to the fleet Grenville had fitted out for Virginia. He probably sailed with them, for in May a letter sent from Plymouth to Drake, then in London, reported 'Here are arrived all the ships from Bristol and all the west parts with Sir Richard Greenfield and Mr St Leger, for which we ...pray your consideration in moneys they demand for victual.' Grenville's ships were his own *Galleon Dudley*, 250 tons, commanded by James Erisey, a distant cousin, and the *Virgin, God Save Her*, 200, under his (Grenville's) son John; the *Bark St Leger*, 160 tons, with his brother-in-law, John St Leger; and probably the *Tiger*, 80 tons, and the *Golden Hind*, 50. By these tonnages, the *Tiger* was obviously not the vessel that had been Grenville's flagship for his first Virginia expedition, nor the *Golden Hind* the famous ship Drake had sailed.

As it happened, it was this smaller *Golden Hind*, commanded by Thomas Fleming, which sighted the Armada off the Lizard in July, and was first back to Plymouth with the news. Grenville was no longer there with his ships, for he had received other orders three months earlier

> Her Majesty considering the danger of this present time and his knowledge and experience in martial affairs, did think it convenient he should remain in those parts to give his assistance and advice to the Lieutenants of Cornwall and Devon.

The news of the Armada's approach was soon spread, presumably by the beacons prepared for the purpose, and the ringing of church bells. When he received the news, Grenville may have been at Stratton, a Cornish manor he had bought in 1576, for local records show that horses were hired there 'to go in post to Launceston for Sr Richard Greinvile to ride to Plimouth when the Spaniards were Come before Plimouth'.[5] The parish also paid 15 pence for two skins to mend a drum 'that was Borrowed for the parish' in case it was necessary to call

50

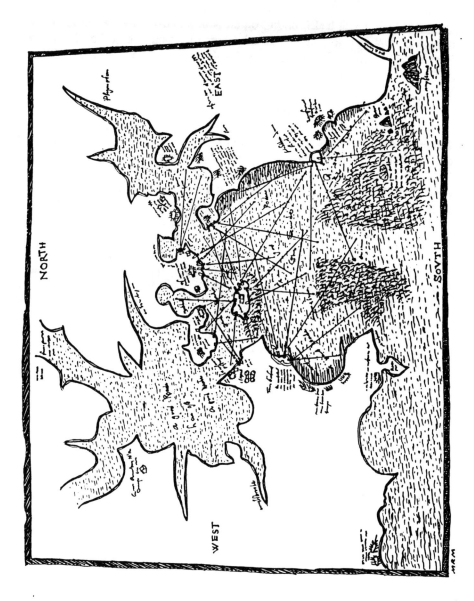

This Chart of Plymouth Sound, inscribed, 'Sr Ric Grenvyle for the fortifying of Plymm', shows possible landing sites, positions of defending troops, local batteries and their fields of fire at the time of the Armada (after a manuscript map in the Public Record Office).

51

out the militia, which had been put on an hour's notice. By the time Grenville arrived at Plymouth to take charge of defence by land if need be, the Spanish fleet had sailed on up-Channel pursued by the English ships, and the militiamen of Devon and Cornwall could lay aside their bows and hackbuts.

Grenville had been given a responsible job, and by all accounts did it well, but in an age when gentlemen craved honour and glory in battle, to say nothing of plunder from captured ships, he must have counted himself unlucky to have been prevented from going to sea. In September however, as some of the returning Spanish ships neared Ireland he was given orders to collect ships and provision them ready to transport soldiers there, lest the Spaniards should land and join forces with the Irish. The Privy Council sent him three royal ships, and in a letter ordering Raleigh to assist him, wrote, 'The ships shall be under the leading of Sir Richard Grenville to use them as he informed to destroy the Spanish ships.' He apparently proposed to use fireships, for the mayor of Bristol was ordered to supply him with 'fifty barrelles of pitch or tarre, five hundred boards, bavin wood [brushwood] and such kinde of stuffe... for her Majesties servyce in Ireland.' These preparations were not necessary in the event, as a good many Spanish ships were driven ashore and wrecked on the west coast of Ireland, and any survivors who did not die of sickness or exposure were rounded up by English troops, or massacred by Irish tribesmen. No Spaniards entered the Irish Sea to threaten the coast of England, and Grenville's small squadron was disbanded, having seen no action and gained no glory.

CHAPTER 10

'The Fight about the Açores'

Grenville spent the years 1589 and 90 on his Irish schemes (chapter 3), but the Spanish war had not ended, and in 1591 he was recalled to the queen's service. Philip II had rebuilt much of his fleet, and now had some large and up-to-date warships to convoy his *flota* or fleet of treasure ships home from the Indies. Few in England realised the new strength of the Spanish fleet, and the squadron sent out under Lord Thomas Howard to the Azores was small. It was probably Raleigh, again prevented from sailing, who had Grenville named as second-in-command.

Grenville sailed in the *Revenge*, of about 500 tons; a royal warship, neither large nor new, having been laid down in 1575. Returning from Ireland in 1582 she ran aground, but was repaired and thoroughly overhauled the next year. She won renown as Drake's ship in the fight against the Armada, when he captured the great Spanish vessel, *Nuestra Senora del Rosario* in the English Channel. On Drake's expedition to Portugal in 1589, the *Revenge* sprung a leak and nearly sank under him, but he somehow managed to bring her home. She had other narrow escapes and was later described by Sir Richard Hawkins as 'ever the most unfortunate ship the late Queen's majesty ever had in her reign'. In spite of this chequered career, however, she had the reputation of being one of the best-armed and fastest sailing vessels in the fleet. She carried about 250 men and 45 guns.

Grenville set off in April 1591, encountered a storm, repaired damage, and went on to capture a large ship of Lubeck laden with masts and plank for Spain, and therefore fair prize. He joined the rest of Howard's squadron off Cape St Vincent, having captured another vessel, and sunk a third. Howard's squadron arrived off the Azores in May, and awaited news of the Spaniards, but they were not only preparing a strong convoy, but delaying the despatch of the *flota*, knowing that the longer the English cruised aimlessly around the islands, the more they would exhaust their supplies, ships, and men. The Spaniards had the best of the long game of cat-and-mouse that summer, for the English, having no Atlantic bases, had nowhere to shelter. Although supplies and reinforcements were sent out, by August many of the men were sick, and the ships in need of overhaul, so towards the end of the month, Howard's squadron, consisting of six or seven medium or small warships, six victuallers and three or four pinnaces,

The Last Fight of the Revenge. *This near-contemporary view, from a tapestry designed by H.C. Vroom and worked in 1598, shows Sir Richard's flagship in the centre foreground. With her foremast shot away, but still thundering defiance, she is flanked by de Bajan's* San Pablo *and the great* San Felipe. *Howard's ships are in flight off Pico near the right horizon; the Spanish fleet is on the left.*

anchored off Flores, one of the westernmost islands of the Azores group.

The English were off guard, with no news of the long-awaited Spanish ships from the west. They did not yet know that an armed convoy sent out from Spain had reached the Azores from the other direction, and knew the whereabouts of the English. The leader was Don Alonso de Bajan, a man of considerable experience at sea, who commanded over 50 vessels carrying 7,000 men, including many soldiers. As soon as the wind allowed, de Bajan ordered his commanders to sail for Flores and surprise the English at anchor. They almost succeeded, but at the last moment, the *Moonshine*, a fast pinnace despatched by the Earl of Cumberland, whose squadron off the Spanish coast had seen de Bajan's fleet put to sea, arrived with news of their approach.

Raleigh, in an account of the action as described to him by survivors, described the scene when the warning was received.

> ...many of our shippes companies were on shore in the Ilande; some providing balast for their ships; others filling of water and refreshing themselves from the land with such things as they could either for money or by force recover. By reason whereof our ships being all pestered and romaging every thing out of order, very light for want of balast, and that which was most to our disadvantage, the one halfe part of the men of every shippe sicke, and utterly unserviceable; for in the *Revenge* there were ninety diseased; in the *Bonaventure* not so many in health as could handle her maine saile... The Spanishe fleet... were now so soone at hand, as our shippes had scarce time to way their anchors, but some of them were driven to let slippe their Cables and set saile.

Considering the odds, Lord Thomas Howard's decision to sail his fleet out of danger was prudent, but Grenville, 'waiting to recover the men that were upon the Island that had otherwise bene lost', was the last to weigh anchor, by which time the leading Spanish ships were upon him, taking his wind. The master, an experienced mariner, told him

> to cut his main sayle, and cast about, and to trust to the sailing of the ship; for the squadron of Sivil were on his weather bow. But Sir Richard utterly refused to turne from the enemie, alleaging that hee would rather choose to die, then to dishonour himselfe, his

countrey, and her Majesties shippe, perswading his companie that hee would passe through two squadrons, in despight of them, and enforce those of Sivil to give him way... In the meane while... the great *San Philip [Felipe]*being in the winde of him, and comming towards him, becalmed his sailes in such sorte, as the shippe could neither make way nor feele the helme; so huge and high carged was the Spanish ship, being of a thousand and five hundred tuns. Who after layd the *Revenge* aboord.

The *Revenge* answered with crossbar shot from the heavy guns of her lower tier, after which the *San Felipe* 'shifted herself with all diligence from her sides, utterly misliking her first entertainment'. The queen's ship *Foresight* took some part in the first two hours of the battle, but withdrew to save herself from being surrounded. The captain of the victualling ship, *George Noble* of London, bravely put himself under Grenville's orders, but was told to save his small vessel. The fight 'continued very terrible all that evening'. The *Revenge* became locked with another huge vessel, the *San Barnabe,* while others, trying to board, crashed not only into the *Revenge*, but each other. The severe damage thus incurred, together with the English broadsides, caused three of the galleons to sink later on, and forced another to run on a beach to save her crew. The Spanish ships

were still repulsed again and again... but as they were wounded and beaten off, so alwayes others came in their places, she never having lesse than two mighty Gallions by her sides and aboard her; So that ere the morning, from three of the clocke the day before, there had been fifteene severall Armadas [armed ships] assayled her.

At dawn, after 15 hours of fighting, the *Revenge,* her masts, rigging, and upperwork all shot away, was a mere hull, leaking, and low in the water. No steering remained, almost all powder was spent, and the pikes with which her crew had resisted boarding parties lay broken. Of the 100 fighting men fit enough for action, 40 had been killed and most of the rest injured. Grenville, who had been shot in the body and head, was mortally wounded, but still on the upper deck, and in command of his faculties. He now proposed, with the help of the master-gunner, to sink the ship in a last grand gesture of defiance, but many on board wanted to save their lives by seeking terms. Grenville refused to surrender, saying 'that the Spaniards should never glory to have taken one shippe of her Majestie, seeing they had so long notably defended themselves'. The other party, however, secretly sent the ship's master to parley. Don Alonso de Bajan, 'finding none over haste to enter the *Revenge* again, doubting least Sir Richard would have blowne them up and himselfe, and perceiving by the report of the Master of the *Revenge* his dangerous disposition' agreed that if the crew surrendered the ship, he would not hand them over to the inquisition or the galleys, but allow them to return to England.

On receiving these terms the crew deserted Grenville and disarmed and locked up the master-gunner, who having been prevented from carrying out Grenville's orders, was trying to kill himself. De Bajan now sent boats to take the *Revenge* and bring Grenville off, 'the ship being marveilous unsavorie, filled with blood and bodies of dead amd wounded men like a slaughter house'. Grenville, 'thus overmatched', contemptuously told his captor that 'hee could doe with his body what he list, for hee esteemed it not'. As he was carried out of the ship he swooned, then reviving, asked the company to pray for him. Although de Bajan, who, according to Raleigh had the greatest admiration for Grenville, 'left nothing unattempted that tended to his recoverie', he died aboard the Spanish flagship, *San Pablo*, two or three days later.

There is another account of Grenville's last few days, written by van Linschoten, a Dutch merchant who was in the Azores at the time of the action, and went aboard one of the Spanish ships soon afterwards. He maintained that after Grenville was brought on board the flagship, de Bajan 'would neither see him or speake to him', which sounds probable, for he had caused great damage to de Bajan's fleet and reputation. To this writer we owe a deathbed scene aboard the *San Pablo*, and Grenville's reputed last words, but Linschoten's information was secondhand, and had probably lost nothing in the telling. An English translation, published a year or two later, omitted Grenville's last sentence as recorded by Linschoten, which, if actually spoken, shows that he had not forgiven his crew for surrendering the *Revenge*. It rings at least as true as the rest.

> ...al the rest of the [Spanish] captaines and gentlemen went to visit him, and to comfort him in his hard fortune, wonderinge at his courage and stout heart, for that he showed not any signe of faintness nor changing of colour; but feeling the houre of death to approach, he spake these words in Spanish and said

> Here die I Richard Greenvil with a joyful and quiet mind, for that I have ended my life as a true soldier ought to do, that hath fought for his countrey, Queene, religion and honor, whereby my soule

most joyful departeth out of this body & shal alwayes leave behind it an everlasting fame of a valiant & true souldier that hath done his dutie as he was bound to doe. But the others of my company have done as traitors and dogs, for which they shall be reproached all their lives and leave a shameful name for ever.

When he had finished these or such other like words he gave up the Ghost with great and stout courage & no man could perceive any true signe of heavines in him.

Most of the English prisoners were distributed among the Spanish fleet, and the hulk of the *Revenge* was taken in tow, a unique trophy to take back to Spain, for she was the only English warship captured up to that time (and, as it turned out, during the whole war). Within a short time, the Spanish ships were joined by many more from the Indies, only to encounter their usual dreadful luck with the weather, as the worst storm of a very turbulent season scattered them, and drove the much-damaged *Revenge* hard ashore at the foot of a cliff, where she 'brake in an hundred pieces & sunke to the ground'. The few English seamen left aboard, and the Spanish prize crew were lost with her. According to Linschoten thousands more Spaniards were drowned or cast ashore, and at least twenty-six of their ships were lost, but by later reports it appears that only about that number reached Spain out of well over one hundred vessels. Raleigh wrote with grim satisfaction

So it pleased them to honor the buriall of that renowned ship the *Revenge*, not suffering her to perish alone, for the great honour she atchieved in her lifetime.

Like a good Englishman, he assumed that 'it hath pleased God to fight for us'; Linschoten, also a protestant, agreed

that it might truely be sayd, the taking of the *Revenge* was justly revenged upon them, amd not by the might and force of men, but by the power of God, as some of them openly sayd... they beleeved verily God would consume them, and that he tooke part with the Lutherans and heretiks: saying that so soone as they had throwen the dead body of the Viceadmiral Sir Richard Greenfield overboard, they verily thought that as he had a divellish faith and religion, and therefore the divels loved him, so he presently sunke to the bottom of the sea, and downe into hell, where he raised up all the divels to the revenge of his death: and that they brought so great stormes and torments upon the Spaniards, because they only maintained the Catholike and Romish religion.

So the Spaniards, unsure whether to blame God or devil, laid their misfortunes at the door of their arch-enemy, Sir Richard Grenville.

A detail from Vroom's painting, 'Storm at Sea', c. 1610. This is thought to portray the great gale off Terceira in which the Revenge *and so many Spanish ships were lost.*

CHAPTER 11

Character and Reputation

> He [Grenville] was of so hard a complexion, that as he continued
> among the Spanish captains while they were at dinner or supper
> with him, he would carouse 3 or 4 glasses of wine, and in a braverie
> take the glasses betweene his teeth and crash them in pieces and
> swalow them downe, so that oftentimes the blood ran out of his
> mouth without any harme at all unto him...

The Dutch merchant, van Linschoten, did not claim to have witnessed this party
trick himself, but wrote that he had heard the tale from several 'credible persons
that many times stood and beheld him'. These were presumably among the
Spaniards with whom the writer was in touch after their fight against the
Revenge - the same people who would soon credit Grenville with conjuring up
devils from hell. The important thing about these stories is not their credibility,
but the fact that they were told at all. They confirm that Sir Richard Grenville
bore a fearsome reputation among his enemies. So did Drake, but he was popular
at home, whereas according to Linschoten, even Grenville's 'own people hated
him for his fierceness, & spake very hardly of him...'

There is little reason to doubt that at the time this was written, Grenville's 'own
people', the survivors of the *Revenge,* hated him, for they had been through a
terrible ordeal, and blamed him for not escaping with the rest of the fleet. Their
story, relayed to Linschoten through his Spanish contacts, was that Grenville
had threatened to hang anyone who tried to sail the ship out of the action, and
was therefore responsible for the battle, the casualties, and the eventual surrender of the *Revenge.* They had a good case, even if Grenville had not used the
threat of hanging; it is easy enough to believe that he had, but Raleigh's account,
which also drew on survivors' evidence does not mention it. It must be
remembered that the men needed to justify themselves, for they had disobeyed
his orders at the last, and according to Linschoten, Grenville with his dying
breath had called them 'traitors and dogs' for surrendering the ship.

The loss of the *Revenge* was bad news at home. In Barnstaple Philip Wyot
recorded in his diary '...her Majesty's ship at sea, Sr Richard Greynfild
Captaine, was taken by the Spaniards after encountring the whole Spanish Fleet
for 2 daies.'[1] In London the government was unwilling to admit defeat, as shown

Sir Richard Grenville in later years, after the engraving by C. van de Passe.

by a letter sent to an English agent in Paris advising him to keep quiet about the loss of the *Revenge*, as they had 'disguised it here with the sinking of so many ships of the King of Spain and loss of so many men...' Rumours were rife, however, and Raleigh, who had backed the expedition and the choice of Grenville as vice-admiral, published his account of the action within a couple of months. In this *Report of the Trueth of the fight about the Isles of the Açores*, Raleigh used his literary skill to make Grenville's undoubted courage transcend his lack of judgement. As with Dunkirk three and a half centuries later, the battle of Flores was turned into virtual victory.

Raleigh, although admitting that flight would have been the better course, considering 'so great an impossibility of prevailing', portrayed Grenville as a great-minded hero who died for queen and country. He thus set the seal on his cousin's reputation, and disarmed the critics who had supported Howard's caution. The story of the 'one and fifty-three' captured and held the admiration of succeeding generations. Bacon compared the stand of the *Revenge* to 'some Heroicall Fable', and when Grenville's widow, Lady Mary died in 1623, the parish clerk of Bideford wrote in the burial register, '...wife of the famous warrior Sir Richard Grenville, Knight... being in his life the Spanniards' Terrour'. Fifty years later the diarist, John Evelyn, sighed, 'Than this what have we more! What can be greater?'.[2]

Writers' opinions of Grenville reflected the ideas of their own times, so in the late eighteenth century, for instance, Grenville was not so much admired. John Watkins, in his essay on Bideford, made no reference to the *Revenge*, but influenced by then-current concepts such as the rights of man, equality, and the 'noble savage', criticised Grenville for his action in laying waste an Indian village, 'pouring depredation and famine upon a whole body for the petty offence of one man... regardless of the principles of natural justice and of the feelings of humanity'.[3] Most people today would echo these sentiments, but soon after Watkins wrote England was saved from invasion by Nelson and the navy, and heroic feats were back in fashion. In the Victorian and Edwardian age of empire Grenville held an unchallenged place in the pantheon of naval heroes, lauded by historians like Froude, and writers like Kingsley, and Tennyson whose epic poem, *The Revenge*, raised hero-worship to even greater heights.

Until recently, apart from certain contemporaries who felt that discretion should have been the better part of valour, and exceptional writers like Watkins, Grenville's critics were few. His historical reputation was mainly based on the dramatic episode that ended his life, and the one criterion of courage in the face of the enemy. In the twentieth century there has been considerable reassessment of the Elizabetham period, and in the present age of the critical historian, Professor Andrews, not afraid to call a pirate a pirate, has blown away some of the clouds of romance, not to say nonsense, that surrounded the 'great seadogs'[4]

To attempt any evaluation of Grenville's character it is necessary to study his whole career in the context of the period, as Dr Rowse has done. The task is made difficult by the loss of family and personal documents, so there is nothing to show whether Grenville was, for instance, a kindly family man. There are some indications that he may have been; there is no evidence that he was unfaithful to his wife, or that he fell out with his half-brothers, who were associated with him in a number of ventures, or with his sons Bernard and John, for both of whom he strove to provide estates. He also remained on good terms with Raleigh and other kinsmen. There are one or two other indications that he was not universally hated, and that some humanity lurked behind the stern front. A young gentleman, sailing on the *Revenge* on her last voyage wrote home full of praise for his 'good usage' at the hands of Sir Richard Grenville, from whom he had received many courtesies.[5] By all accounts too, it was Grenville who insisted on staying behind at Flores to take the sick men on board to save them from the inquisition or the galleys. These things apart, it has to be acknowledged that Grenville as a public figure, leader, and man of action, appeared to be, as Linschoten wrote, 'of nature very severe'.

Grenville's severity was apparent throughout his career; he must have been a difficult and frightening man to cross. He acted forcibly, and sometimes rashly, especially when his temper was roused. He mortally wounded an adversary in a quarrel even before he came of age. He also savagely repressed Irish rebels, persecuted English Catholics, plundered ships, threatened to hang prisoners, burnt an Indian settlement, quarrelled with subordinate officers. Some of these actions, taken in their context, were justified by the standards of the times and the dangers to the country. Moreover, Grenville's behaviour was by no means unique. Similar lists of excesses could be made for Drake, Hawkins, Gilbert, Frobisher and others. They were men of action in situations where it was often necessary to kill or be killed, command or be overthrown. Raleigh committed similar acts on the occasions when he was in the front line, and condoned and profited from them when he was not.

Grenville did not possess Raleigh's panache, and lacked the common touch which made Drake popular. He was loyal, thorough, effective, and unfailing in his duty, but there was little to lighten his severity. He had the reputation, even in his own time, as the proudest, fiercest, and most warlike Elizabethan of all.

SOURCES AND REFERENCES

To avoid repetition and overuse of footnotes in a small book, the main sources for each chapter are listed first. Quotations from these are not separately referenced. Other quotations and references are noted as they occur.

ABBREVIATIONS

CSPD	Calendar of State Papers, Domestic
CTS	Catholic Truth Society
DAT	Devonshire Association Transactions
DCRS	Devon and Cornwall Record Society
ESH	Exeter Studies in History
IPM	Inquisition *Post Mortem*
NDRO	North Devon Record Office
PRO	Public Record Office
WCSL	West Country Studies Library, Exeter

Chapter 1

Roger Granville, *The History of the Granville Family* (Exeter 1895), chapters 1-5.

A. L. Rowse, *Sir Richard Grenville of the Revenge* (1937), chapters 1-2.

1. WCSL, IPM Transcripts; Roger Granville 1523; Sir Richard Granville 1550.

2. Roger Granville, *The King's General in the West* (1908), 7; O J Reichel, *Devon Feet of Fines*, I (DCRS 1912), 41 (no.69).

3. John Watkins, *An Essay towards a History of Bideford* (Exeter 1792), 12-15.

4. R. Dew, *A History of the Parish and Church of Kilkhampton* (2nd edition, 1928), 2-5.

5. J. A. Youings, *Devon Monastic Lands - Calendar of Particulars for Grants 1536-1558* (DCRS, New Series I, 1955), 18-19.

6. Richard Carew of Antony, *The Survey of Cornwall* (ed. F. E. Halliday 1953), 180.

7. Carew, *Cornwall*, 134.

8. Margaret Rule, *The Mary Rose* (1982), 36-8.

Chapter 2

Granville, *Granville Family*, chapter 6.

Rowse, *Grenville*, chapter 3.

1. Carew, *Cornwall*, 134.

Chapter 3

K. S. Bottigheimer, 'Kingdom and colony: Ireland in the Westward Enterprise 1536-1660' in K. R. Andrews, N. P. Canny and P. E. H. Nair (eds.), *The Westward Enterprise: English Activities in Ireland, the Atlantic and America, 1480-1650* (Liverpool, 1978), 45-64.

Rowse, *Grenville*, chapters 3 and 15.

1. K. R. Andrews, *Trade, Plunder and Settlement* (Cambridge 1984), 184.

2. Andrews, *Trade, Plunder and Settlement*, 185.

3. Andrews, *Trade, Plunder and Settlement*, 186; Rowse, *Grenville*, 160-1.

4. W. Shakespeare, *King Henry the Fifth*, Act III, Scene III, 33-40.

Chapter 4

R. Pearse Chope, 'New light on Sir Richard Grenville, I', *DAT* 49 (1917), 210-246.

Rowse, *Grenville*, chapter 5.

1. Andrews, *Trade, Plunder and Settlement*, 149.

Chapter 5

C. Gill, *Buckland Abbey* (Revised Edition, Plymouth, 1963).

Rowse, *Grenville*, chapters 6 and 9.

Watkins, *Bideford*, 18-27.

1. R. Pearse Chope, Letter to *Western Morning News*, June 1928.

2. NDRO, Bideford Parish Registers of Baptisms (1588) and Burials (1589).

3. An account of 1588, by John White, cited in R. Pearse Chope, 'New light on

Sir Richard Grenville', II *DAT* 49 (1917), 278, mentions Clovelly Quay. As it existed at that date it is possible that Cary, who had it built, had discussed its construction with Grenville.

4. Rowse, *Grenville*, 256.

5. Rowse, *Grenville*, 56, 76-7, 149, 160, 232.

6. B. Cherry and N. Pevsner, *The Buildings of England: Devon* (2nd edition, 1989), 227-9.

7. J. A. Youings, 'Drake, Grenville and Buckland Abbey', *DAT* 112 (1980), 95-9.

Chapter 6

P. A. Boyan (compiler), *Blessed Cuthbert Mayne* (CTS 1961), *passim.*

Rowse, *Grenville*, chapter 7.

Chapter 7

K. R. Andrews, 'Elizabethan privateering', in *Raleigh in Exeter 1985* (ESH 10, Exeter, 1985), 1-20.

Richard Hakluyt, *The Principal Navigations, Voyages, Traffiques and Discoveries of the English Nation*, 6 (Everyman 1907, rpt. 1926), 132-8.

Pearse Chope, 'Sir Richard Grenville,' II, 247-82.

D. B. Quinn, *The Roanoke Voyages 1584-1590*, 2 vols. (Cambridge, Hakluyt Society, Second Series 104 (1952), I, 461-88; II, 555-62.

Rowse, *Grenville,* chapters 7 and 8.

1. PRO, E190, 935/9, Exchequer King's Remembrancer Port Book for Barnstaple (including Bideford), Michaelmas 1588 - Michaelmas 1589.

2. I. Friell, 'The three-masted ship and Atlantic voyages', in *Raleigh in Exeter 1985*, 32.

3. Rowse, *Grenville*, 69.

4. Rowse, *Grenville*, 218-9.

5. P. Wyot, *Diary 1586-1606*, in J. R. Chanter, *Sketches of the Literary History of Barnstaple* (Barnstaple 1866), 92.

Chapter 8

Hakluyt, *Principal Navigations*, 6, 132-8, 159-64.

Pearse Chope, 'Sir Richard Grenville', II, 247-82.

Quinn, *Roanoke Voyages*, 461-70, 475-76.

D. B. Quinn, *Set Fair for Roanoke* (Chapel Hill 1985), chapters 5, 6, and 10.

Rowse, *Grenville*, chapters 10-13.

1. Rowse, *Grenville*, 203.

2. Andrews, *Trade, Plunder and Settlement*, 196-7.

3. *CSPD 1581-90*, 323.

4. Wyot, *Diary*, 91.

Chapter 9

Pearse Chope, 'Sir Richard Grenville', II, 247-82.

Rowse, *Grenville*, chapter 14.

J. A. Youings, 'Bowmen, Billmen and Hackbutters: the Elizabethan Militia in the South West', in R. Higham (ed.), *Security and Defence in South-West England before 1800* (ESH 19, Exeter, 1987), 51-68.

1. Wyot, *Diary*, 94.

2. *CSPD 1581-90,* 140, 323. Wyot, *Diary*, 93.

3. Hakluyt, *Principal Navigations*, 6, 207.

4. Wyot, *Diary*, 94.

5. Rowse, *Grenville*, 128.

Chapter 10

J. H. van Linschoten, *A Large Testimony...*, in Hakluyt, *Principal Navigations,* 5, 36-43.

Sir W. Raleigh, *A Report of the Trueth of the Fight about the Isles of the Açores 1591*, in Hakluyt, *Principal Navigations*, V, 5-15.

Rowse, *Grenville*, chapter 17.

Chapter 11

Linschoten, *A Large Testimony...*

Raleigh, *...Fight about the Isles of the Açores.*

Rowse, *Grenville*, chapter 18.

1. Wyot, *Diary*, 98

2. NDRO, Bideford Parish Register of Burials (1623); Pearse Chope, 'Sir Richard Grenville', I, 210; J. Evelyn, Navigation and Commerce (1674), 76, cited in G. H. Bushnell, *Sir Richard Grenville* (1936), 315.

3. Watkins, *Bideford,* 57.

4. K. R. Andrews, 'Elizabethan privateering', in *Raleigh in Exeter 1985*, 1-20.

5. Rowse, *Grenville,* 298.

THE REVENGE

by Alfred Lord Tennyson

At Flores in the Azores Sir Richard Grenville lay,
And a pinnace, like a fluttered bird, came flying from far away,
"Spanish ships of war at sea! we have sighted fifty-three!"
Then sware Lord Thomas Howard : "'Fore God I am no coward;
But I cannot meet them here, for my ships are out of gear,
And the half my men are sick. I must fly, but follow quick.
We are six ships of the line; can we fight with fifty-three?"

Then spake Sir Richard Grenville : "I know you are no coward;
You fly them for a moment to fight with them again.
But I've ninety men and more that are lying sick ashore.
I should count myself the coward if I left them, my Lord Howard,
To these Inquisition dogs and the devildoms of Spain."

So Lord Howard passed away with five ships of war that day,
Till he melted like a cloud in the silent summer heaven;
But Sir Richard bore in hand all his sick men from the land,
Very carefully and slow,
Men of Bideford in Devon,
And we laid them on the ballast down below;
For we brought them all aboard,
And they blest him in their pain, that they were not left to Spain,
To the thumbscrew and the stake, for the glory of the Lord.

He had only a hundred seamen to work the ship and to fight,
And he sailed away from Flores till the Spaniard came in sight,
With his huge sea-castles heaving upon the weather bow.
"Shall we fight or shall we fly?
Good Sir Richard, tell us now,
For to fight is but to die!
There'll be little of us left by the time this sun be set."

And Sir Richard said again : "We be all good English men.
Let us bang these dogs of Seville, the children of the devil,
For I never turned my back upon Don or devil yet."

Sir Richard spoke, and he laughed, and we roared a hurrah, and so
The little Revenge ran on sheer into the heart of the foe,
With her hundred fighters on deck, and her ninety sick below;
For half their fleet to the right and half to the left were seen,
And the little Revenge ran on through the long sea-lane between.

Thousands of their soldiers looked down from their decks and laughed,
Thousands of their seamen made mock at the mad little craft,
Running on and on, till delayed
By their mountain-like San Philip that, of fifteen hundred tons,
And up-shadowing high above us with her yawning tiers of guns,
Took the breath from our sails, and we stayed.

And while now the great San Philip hung above us like a cloud
Whence the thunderbolt will fall
Long and loud,
Four galleons drew away
From the Spanish fleet that day,
And two upon the larboard and two upon the starboard lay,
And the battle thunder broke from them all.
But anon the great San Philip, she bethought herself and went,
Having that within her womb that had left her ill content;
And the rest they came aboard us, and they fought us hand to hand,
For a dozen times they came with their pikes and musqueteers,
And a dozen times we shook 'em off as a dog that shakes his ears
When he leaps from the water to the land.

And the sun went down, and the stars came out far over the summer sea
But never a moment ceased the fight of the one and the fifty-three.
Ship after ship, the whole night long, their high-built galleons came,
Ship after ship, the whole night long, with her battle-thunder and flame;
Ship after ship, the whole night long, drew back with her dead and her
    shame.
For some were sunk and many were shattered, and so could fight us no
    more -
God of battles, was ever a battle like this in the world before?

For he said, "Fight on! fight on!"
Though his vessel was all but a wreck;
And it chanced that, when half of the short summer night was gone,
With a grisly wound to be drest he had left the deck,
But a bullet struck him that was dressing it suddenly dead,
And himself he was wounded again in the side and the head,
And he said, "Fight on! fight on!"

And the night went down and the sun smiled out far over the summer sea,
And the Spanish fleet with broken sides lay round us all in a ring;
But they dared not touch us again, for they feared that we still could sting,
So they watched what the end would be.
And we had not fought them in vain,
But in perilous plight were we,
Seeing forty of our poor hundred were slain,
And half of the rest of us maimed for life
In the crash of the cannonades and the desperate strife;
And the sick men down in the hold were most of them stark and cold,
And the pikes were all broken or bent, and the powder was all of it spent;
And the masts and the rigging were lying over the side;

But Sir Richard cried in his English pride :
"We have fought such a fight for a day and a night
As may never be fought again!
We have won great glory, my men!
And a day less or more
At sea or ashore,
We die - does it matter when?
Sink me the ship, Master Gunner - sink her, split her in twain!
Fall into the hands of God, not into the hands of Spain!"

And the gunner said, "Ay, ay," but the seamen made reply:
"We have children, we have wives,
And the Lord hath spared our lives.
We will make the Spaniard promise, if we yield, to let us go;
We shall live to fight again and to strike another blow."
And the lion there lay dying, and they yielded to the foe.

And the stately Spanish men to their flagship bore him then,
Where they laid him by the mast, old Sir Richard caught at last,

And they praised him to his face with their courtly foreign grace;
But he rose upon their decks, and he cried:
"I have fought for Queen and Faith like a valiant man and true;
I have only done my duty as a man is bound to do;
With a joyful spirit I Sir Richard Grenville die!"
And he fell upon their decks and he died.

And they stared at the dead that had been so valiant and true,
And had holden the power and glory of Spain so cheap
That he dared her with one little ship and his English few;
Was he devil or man? He was devil for aught they knew,
But they sank his body with honour down into the deep,
And they manned the Revenge with a swarthier alien crew,
And away she sailed with her loss and longed for her own;

When a wind from the lands they had ruined awoke from sleep,
And the water began to heave and the weather to moan,
And or ever that evening ended a great gale blew,
And a wave like the wave that is raised by an earthquake grew,
Till it smote on their hulls and their sails and their masts and their flags,
And the whole sea plunged and fell on the shot-shattered navy of Spain,
And the little Revenge herself went down by the island crags
To be lost evermore in the main.

INDEX OF MAIN PEOPLE, PLACES, AND EVENTS

LIST OF SUBSCRIBERS

Revd. Dr Richard Acworth
Joyce and Alex Andrew
Mrs I Arkle
Evelyn M Attwood
Mrs N Badcock
D O Bailey
G F Bailey
Mrs C Bain
William M Ball
J Barber
Tom C P Bartlett
D Beara
Lt Cdr John W Beck RN
Monica M Becket
Miss M L Beer
Noel Beer
Mike Bender
Bideford Bay Amateur Radio Club
Mr Allan John Bissett
John Blowey
Alexander Boulter
Thomas Boulter
Mrs V J Boyle
Miss E Brain
W R Bray
Harriet Bridle
J F J Broad
Martin Bucknell
J C Campbell
Captain John Cann
Elizabeth Chambers
Dick Chandler
R E Channing
Peter Christie
Dorothy Cleaver
David B Clement
W L and E B Cobbledick
D J B Coulter
Courtney Library, Royal Institution of Cornwall

Mr & Mrs W P Cox
Miss M H Culham
Winifred Currie
Ian Dacre-Merry
Peter J Darke, AFC, FCIS.
Susan M Dart
J G Davies
Paul D J Davies
Mary de la Mahotiere
Devon and Exeter Institution Library
Devon County Library
Richard J Digweed
Mr J Dilley
Mrs B Dixon
Mary Dobson
Mrs Ruth Dunstan
Edgehill College, Junior Department
David Edmund
Colin Elliott
Exeter Rare Books
Peter Ferguson
Mrs Richard Meyrick Flemington
Peggy Fletcher
Chris and Roy Foster
R W Forward
Betty and Barney Francis
H Norman Fulford
Paul A Gainey
K L and P Gardner
Matthew J Gentry
Mrs Joan Gill
R Girling
Miss N D Goodwin
Richard Granville
Todd Gray
Richard Grenville de C Grenfell-Hill
Alan Grenville Ford
Mr Leslie Gray
M Guegan

Pamela Harper
Heather Harrower
T M C Hay
B W Higgs
Mr and Mrs J A Bruce Hoare
J K Hoare
R S & E P Hobson
D C Hocking
Alan Hogan
T D Hooper
Barry Hughes
Sheila L Hutchinson
J A and H G Huish
George W Isaac
Mr D E Ivall
Mrs S Ivatts
Miss D M I Jackson
Mary Johnson
Pat Jolliffe
Roy Kennington
C M Keirnander
A R Killick
Barbara and Dennis Kitchen
R E Loder
Dr G M Longfield-Jones
Mrs G M Love
V Marklew
Stephen Marriage
Miss Margaret Matthews
David M Maxwell
Col. M W Maxse
Cdr J A McPhee
Bernard Mead
June Meadows
N T P Metcalfe
P G Mills
W J Moase
Mr and Mrs D C Moore
J Mothersole
Alex C Munro-Chick
F Murley
Mark Myers

Emma Nicholson MP
North Devon Athenaeum
John Nunn
Miss Elizabeth Paddon
Mrs S A Palmer
Mr F and Mrs A R Parkhouse
W A Passmore
Alan Pearson
Mrs C J Phillips
R Phillips
Jack and Kay Pinkett
Alan and Anne Pitcher
Miss C M Pothan
D A Proctor
Mrs Evelyn Puddicombe
A H Reed
Margaret Reed
N H Rendell-Reynolds
Mr G Richards
Mrs D I Rickard
Louise Rose
Timothy John Ruck
Jonathan P Rumball
Pearl St Ville
Tony and Helen Saltern
Mrs J M Sedgwick
Jack Sharp
Dr D C Shields
Mrs P M Slade
Miss Helen Slocombe
Mr L R Smale
Mrs M F Snetzler
Dr Donald R Snow
Richard Southern
Frank Spiegelhalter
Patricia E Squires
Miss M Stacey
Miss Una Stock
James Stratten
R V Tait
A J N Tamlyn
Sheila M Tilley

Subscribers *(continued)*

Paul Tipping
Frank Turner
Mrs M A Van der Heyden
Lady Walker
S Wall
Joanne Waters
Merran Waters
Mr & Mrs T J Waters

Julian Wedgewood
Ian J Whitfield
Pat & Tom Wiggett
Mrs S Willis
Edward & Barbara Virgo
Mrs D M Yendell
H R F Young